3D

First published 2006
by Laundrette Books

Copyright © 2006 retained by individual authors
Compilation © 2006 Laundrette Books

All rights reserved.
No part of this publication may be reproduced, stored in a retrieval system, or transmitted in any form or by any means without the prior permission in writing of the respective author, nor be otherwise circulated in any form of binding or cover other than that in which it is published and without similar condition including this condition being imposed on the subsequent purchaser.

Printed and bound in Great Britain
by Russell Press, Nottingham

Printed on Crossbow paper
Minimum 20% post consumer fibre
80% virgin fibre from fully sustainable, managed forest

Laundrette Books
Nottingham Trent University
Clifton Lane
Nottingham
NG11 8NS

Acknowledgements

Thanks to Andrew Short for proof reading and tea supplies. To Maxine Linnell, Elaine Kazmierczuk, Frances Thimann and Anne Holloway for final editing support. Thanks to editing teams, Marcus Saban, Fay Watkins, Lynda Blagg, Phil Bond, Maiko Nagamori and Vicky. Huge thanks to Diana Peasey for publicity and reading arrangements and Sally Morten for being involved with everything! To Lynda for additional illustrations, and to Ian Douglas for the cover design and help with art team. To David Belbin for constant support and advice. And to Russell Press for answering last minute questions and for putting it all together.

Thank you all.

Karen Duncan.

School of Arts, Communication and Culture
Creative Writing...be inspired

So you want to be a writer? On the MA in Creative Writing at Nottingham Trent University you will be inspired by professional writers to advance your own writing talent.

This practical postgraduate course is run entirely by successful writers with long-term experience of the publishing industry. It is suitable for students with a talent for and commitment to creative writing, and many of our students have acquired agents and publishing deals.

Alongside the core writing module and dissertation you can choose options in Children's and Young Adult Fiction, Creative Non-Fiction, Fiction, Poetry and Scriptwriting.

New for 2006

We are delighted to announce the appointment of two new visiting professors to the MA in Creative Writing:

David Almond (Whitbread Children's Book Award winner)
Michael Eaton MBE (distinguished TV scriptwriter)

"Doing the MA gave me an excuse to concentrate on my writing, and take my ambitions seriously. I don't doubt that what I learnt helped me get published quicker."
Nicola Monaghan's *The Killing Jar* was published by Chatto and Windus in 2006.

**For more information call 0115 848 3136
or email acc.postgrad@ntu.ac.uk**

www.ntu.ac.uk/MACreative

NOTTINGHAM
TRENT UNIVERSITY

Contents

Emily's Room – *Simon Dawes*……………………….…..1

The Music And Her Voice – *Maiko Nagamori* ………..7
    Illustration by Amiko Kitamura

Your Birds And Your Fish – *Erika Martin*…………..14
    Illustration by Maureen Bellamy

Tiger Moth – *Graham Joyce*……………………….....15

Sleeping Beauty – *Roberta J Dewa*………………….27

The Real Thing – *Lynda Blagg*……………....……...32
    Illustration by Lynda Blagg

Eggs – *Mahendra Solanki*……………………………38

Cracking – *Jennie Wallace*………………………….39

Revolving Doors: A Prison Diary – *Phil Bond*…....…45

It's Saturday Night – *Maxine Linnell*…..…………...51

A Pigeon In The Attic – *Rosemary Brierley*…………55
    Illustration by Ian Douglas

Shoe – *Anne Holloway*………………………………62

Don't Do Voodoo – *Toby Malamute*…………………65

The Mad Man In The Attic - *Louise Slocombe*………71

Pillow Talk – *Ian Douglas*……………………………76
    Illustration by Ian Douglas

Letter Of The Law – *Loay Hady*………………....….78

Untitled – *Emma O'Brien*...81

Photographs – *Frances Thimann*..................................86

Beer And Bombs – *Ian Douglas*...................................93

Transit – *Diana Peasey*..97

Selective Living – *Fay Watkins*..................................100

How Did That Get There – *Ronan Fitzsimons*............105

Before 1963 – *John Lucas*...113

The Human Mind's Remarkable Ability To Remove Itself – *Adam E Smith*..114
    Illustration by Robbie Smith

Nets – *David Belbin*..119

Joshy Sleeping – *Erika Martin*...................................124
    Illustration by Emily Jane McPherson

Metamorphosis – *Nicola Monaghan*..........................125

Compline – *Elaine Kazmierczuk*................................130

Self Uncondemned – *Peter Porter*.............................131

Gabbro – *Marcus Saban*..132

Cover illustration by Ian Douglas

EMILY'S ROOM

Simon Dawes

Julia ceased weeping against her daughter's bed and held her breath as she listened to him turning his key in the door. She had been crouched on the floor all afternoon, sobbing into the duvet since coming home, having run straight upstairs and into Emily's room. On any other day she would have walked straight through to the kitchen to make herself a much needed tea, which she would have drunk leisurely at the breakfast table whilst half-listening to a programme on the radio. She allowed herself a break prior to the mid-afternoon rush to get some housework done before three thirty. On any other day, Emily would be waiting to be picked up from school. Today, though, she would not be picking Emily up.

Robert, her husband, called out for her, and closed the front door behind him. She listened to him walking into the living room, then out again and down the hall into the kitchen. He called for her again when he had come back to stand at the foot of the stairs. She thought of the lock on the door to the bathroom, and wished that she'd been in there instead. She hadn't even closed the bedroom door. As Robert flicked the switch downstairs, light came into the room from the landing. How could she speak to him, what on earth could she say?

They had redecorated Emily's room just three months ago. Gone were the gender-neutral tones they'd opted for the last time it had been done. The room was now very pink and very much that of a stereotypical girl. And despite their best efforts to avoid buying her dolls and more dolls every birthday or forcing her to take ballet lessons, Emily had resisted by conforming to every cliché of femininity. Her leotard and ballet shoes, and her jodhpurs and riding boots, were ceremoniously placed at opposing corners of the room. Nothing horrified her more than Robert suggesting they take a ball with them to the park. Having fitted a carpet that was a few shades of pink lighter than the colour of the walls, they had made the room give the impression of being bigger than it actually was, or at least bigger than it had previously appeared. Clothes and opened CD-single cases were strewn across the width of the room (she'd had friends round the previous evening). Julia supposed it looked much like any other girl's room. Posters of singers in boy bands, of footballers (her sole concession to Robert's efforts to introduce her to the sport) and of actors from TV and Hollywood, adorned the walls, hiding some of the pink. Julia's own childhood room, she reflected, had looked more or less the same. She remembered crying in that room then as a child, as she cried in this one now.

And she remembered holidays on caravan parks, summers at the beach, images of Emily riding her bike and playing in the sand. Images of herself as a child - memories of photos, perhaps – doing similar things, or standing dutifully in swimming costume beside aunts now dead and gone, and cousins long forgotten. With some of the images it was difficult to tell if it was Emily or herself she was picturing. While they had always taken Emily to Bournemouth, Julia's own childhood memories were from Skegness. They were just pictures of a happy child, either her or Emily. One beach looked much like any other to her. Robert had always hated Skegness, and, consequently, Emily had never seen it. Emily had looked a lot like she had as a child. Over the past couple of years the consensus seemed to be shifting to the opinion that Emily had her father's eyes, his nose, something of her father about her. Julia disagreed, and would often bring out her parents' old photo albums to disprove the consensus. They both had the same flat, light brown hair, and the same undeniable chink in the tip of the nose, she would argue. She remembered having always been paranoid about how noticeable her chink was, though to her recollection, nobody, before Robert, had ever commented upon it. He told her repeatedly how much he adored her nose, and always conceded that he thought Emily looked more like her than she did him. He dismissed with a shrug and a reassuring smile the views to the contrary of everyone else they knew.

Last year they had gone to the south of France. They had stayed in a chalet with Julia's parents, who had never been abroad. Unless you counted the places in which her father had served during the war. She had only a vague memory of the few arguments they'd had with her parents on that holiday, and the tensions that inevitably surfaced every time conversation turned to politics. Her father had never approved of their decision to send Emily to a private school, and she disapproved of the way he talked about immigrants in front of Emily. But her memories of that holiday were fond ones. Even though she couldn't recall many moments of merriment, every scene was a happy one that brought a nostalgic smile to her face. Family was important to her, and she enjoyed having everyone there together. Mum and Dad had made the most of the week by spoiling Emily with affection, who in turn, had basked in the attention showered upon her, and the week had flown by. Julia and Robert had the space to spend some quality time with each other while Emily took advantage of the goodwill of her grandparents. And though it couldn't be said that Julia had ever really looked forward to seeing either her interfering mother or her brooding father, having them close and knowing that they were always there for her if she needed them, had been an anchor in her life; given her a sense of security. Since they had died, that security had been missing from her life, and she lived in fear of something happening to either Robert or Emily. She wished now that she could go back to her parents' house, run up the stairs and shut herself up in her old room. Her mum would have come in to comfort her. She'd have had to go to her dad for comfort, he'd never have made the first move, but he'd have given her that comfort, as much as she needed, without a moment's hesitation. She pictured the exterior of that old terraced house. Now it belonged to someone who owned half the street and let his properties out to students. She couldn't go back to the home she'd spent eighteen years growing up in. It was with hopeless desperation that she wished for her mother to come in now and put her arms around her, or for her father to be hovering about downstairs, knowing there was something wrong but not knowing exactly what to do. If she were to run downstairs, she would see the relief and empathy on his face, and his arms unfolding for her to run into.

"Julia!"

Robert mounted the stairs, calling her name with every third or fourth step. He knew she was in the house. Of course he did, her car was on the drive. And where else would she have been? She had hoped to remain there undiscovered, praying that he would walk past the room without thinking of checking. Leaving her in peace, curled up on the floor with her head against the side of the child's bed. She considered hiding, underneath the bed or on the other side of it, but she didn't move. How desperately she wanted not to speak, but to be left alone.

Her thoughts turned to Emily. Poor Emily. She had always been such a sensitive, fragile child, as Julia had been when she was growing up. To compensate, she had always been especially conscious of the need to protect her daughter, to reassure her that they would always be there. Robert often accused her of being overprotective, said that her wrapping the child in cotton wool all the time was what made her so sensitive. But she would never forget that time in Bournemouth when Emily went missing and Robert showed a different side, showed that he did care and that he too understood the need to protect their daughter. They'd been staying in a caravan on a park near the beach, on holiday with her sister's family and their parents. The beach was overcrowded, and it was too hot to stay outside for long. It took a few minutes of searching the horizon for them to spot the children, who had gone off playing, among the rocks on the shore. Once the kids had seen their parents waving at them and motioning to come back across the beach, they had dutifully returned to have more sunscreen rubbed on their backs. When they came back without Emily, not knowing where she'd gone, Julia had become hysterical. She and Robert had taken one direction, her sister and brother-in-law another, while her Mum and Dad had stayed back at the caravan with the kids. She remembered how strong Robert had been. How he had taken control of the situation and recognised the need to act immediately. He would ask everyone they passed on the beach if they had seen a little girl of Emily's description, which direction she had gone in, shouting so that as many people as possible could hear him. He phoned the police with his mobile and gave clear and concise answers to the person on the other end of the line, while all the time stressing the urgency of the matter. These were the actions of somebody who was normally incapable of asking questions of strangers, certainly of asking for help. He was habitually reluctant to phone the police, insisting that there was never any point. He had surprised her that day. She had been able to depend on him. When a police officer finally found Emily still wandering amongst the windbreakers and beach towels, it was to Robert that she was grateful. She couldn't even picture the officer's face.

"Julia!" He waited, then knocked on the bathroom door (it must have been closed). He called again (probably certain that she was inside), his voice sounding softer and more concerned, before turning the handle and opening the door. Julia heard him sigh impatiently through his teeth as he opened the door. He had a habit of making such sighs, mannerisms which Julia often mimicked, much to his annoyance. He rarely showed signs of anger, was never violent, but he did sigh constantly through each day.

"Julia!" Louder now, though still restrained, his steps quicker and heavier. Julia visualised him striding into the master bedroom, their bedroom, turning on the light and scanning the room for signs that she had been there recently. She remembered the green dress she'd tried on and discarded that morning. He'd probably see it hanging off the edge of their bed. Steps again as he walked towards Emily's room. As his hand slapped against the bedroom door, as it swung open, Julia remarked to herself that he hadn't bothered to turn off the light in their room, something he was always criticising her for not doing.

"Are you alright?" he asked, instinctively. "What on earth are you doing in here?" She turned to look up at him. "And why didn't you answer me? I've been calling you for ages." He seemed to be frozen in the position he'd been in when he'd finally found her, his arm still perpendicular to his body and supporting him against the wall, his index finger outstretched and pressing down firmly on the light switch. The lower part of his forearm extended beyond the cuff of his jacket sleeve, revealing his strength, the darkness of his skin, the thickness of the hair that spread to the back of his hands. He looked around at the room. His heavy eyebrows furrowed and met in the middle, and his protruding forehead wrinkled into four or five distinct levels. "And where's Emily?"

Julia bowed her head and tried to control her breathing. She was suddenly overcome with the need to sob again, and wanted to say what she had to say without bursting into tears.

"Where's Emily?" he asked again, more urgently this time.

"She's at my sister's," Julia answered, her voice weak, barely audible. "I asked her to pick her up for me."

She couldn't look him in the face without feeling as if she was going to be sick. Her throat felt blocked and her chest felt heavily weighed upon. The thought that her heart was broken came to mind, but it wasn't her heart. It was the life she had built for herself. She looked around at the bedroom again, at her daughter's bedroom, their daughter's bedroom. At the signs of love everywhere. At all the things they had bought for her, that had been accumulated over her life. All the things that belonged to her, that expressed the person she was, that expressed who she was going to be. Their daughter. The child of their happy family.

"I know about you and Angela," Julia said, finally; her voice much more confident now, distilled of emotion, matter of fact. Robert didn't say anything. Nor did he move for a while. Eventually his arm dropped from the wall and hung loosely at his side. She looked up at him again, and he avoided her gaze, bowing his head as she continued to stare at him, and as she wondered what would happen now.

She wanted to know what people did when something like this happened. She wanted to know where their family stood now. Whether she could go on as his wife, knowing that he had cheated on her? She wanted to know why, and for how long the affair had been going on. But more importantly, she wanted to know what to do. What she was supposed to do. Her husband, her charming, well-meaning husband had been sleeping with another woman. She didn't know why, for how long, or how to deal with it. And she wanted to know how they would tell Emily. If they would tell Emily.

Robert spoke, he apologised, he explained. He came towards her, knelt down in front of her and held her hands, tears welling up in his eyes as he spoke softly to her. After a while he sat down on the floor beside her, his back against Emily's bed. His head sank into the colourful bed sheets.

THE MUSIC AND HER VOICE

Maiko Nagamori

The ride back home seemed as though it would never end. It had been more than half a day on the plane, staying over in a hotel for the night, hurrying onto the train in the morning and another six hours of long distance bus travel. Mei wondered if she was riding on a weekday or the weekend. The back of her body was aching. She could no longer take the jostling of the vehicle but the journey was almost over. She got off the bus and into a taxi.

She sighed with relief as a beautiful mansion came into view. The green, immaculately cut lawn led up to the entrance. A few cars were parked, some were familiar, belonging to the residents. The others belonged to guests. Her taxi went through the barred, heavy gate and turned left. It kept going straight then turned right. Mei glanced out of the window. The relief of getting off the transport soon subsided, and was taken over by anxiety as she came to view a small wooden house. It looked more like a cottage. She saw someone moving by the window but the next moment the figure quickly disappeared. Mei held her breath, but let it out instantly and deliberately. Control the fear, be strong, do not act like a child and focus.

Stepping out of the taxi she felt the dense, warm air of the countryside. Looking up, thick clouds completely blocked the sun. Her attempt to stand up straight failed, she winced, rubbing her back gently with her hand. It was stiff, one of the bones seemed to be sticking out. She promised herself to take a long bath and stretch out later. She took the first bag to the door. In a rhythmic but slow movement, she took the other bags one by one. Last, she picked up her cello, walked to the door and turned the knob. As expected, it was open so she went in and set the cello inside the corridor. She placed the bags next to the cello and advanced to the kitchen. Her mother was standing by the window with the kettle on.

"I am back, Mother." She felt irritated to hear her voice tremble slightly, she was sure her mother had noticed. A tall thin woman with silky black hair, she turned around to face her daughter. With a smile Sue made the gesture of welcoming. Her mouth was only partly smiling. Mei felt her mother's eyes pierce through hers. A familiar chilling sensation took place. Sue stepped forward and gave her rigid daughter a swift hug. Mei had no time to respond, feeling her bony arms touch hers and thought how frail her mother was. The smell of her mother's hair was both comforting and disturbing. Instead of hugging back, she stood there like a mannequin. Her mother gestured her to sit down and continued with the kettle. Mei obeyed instantly and sat down. Sue poured the hot water into an ancient teapot. She set the pot in the middle of the table followed by two cups.

Mei simply followed the movement of her mother's fingers in silence. Her mother placed one cup in front of her and took the other. The fresh smell of the oolong tea filled her lungs. She took a couple of deep breaths before touching the cup. Her mother sipped the tea slowly. Mei took the cup with both hands and drank it. Despite the fresh welcoming smell, the bitterness and the heat made her choke and she coughed a few times. Sue continued to sip her tea while she studied her coughing daughter. Mei looked down at the cup to avoid looking at her mother. For a long time mother and daughter sipped their tea.

Finally Mei began to talk about her journey. She talked about the long days on the train, places she had visited. She explained about the competition. Mei noticed that her mother's hand quivered at the mention of it so she stopped abruptly. A long silence followed. In that silence, Mei struggled to start another conversation. She opened her mouth several times. On the other hand Sue seemed to be caught up in her own mind; she did nothing to encourage her daughter to continue. In the end, Mei thanked her for the tea and took her cello up to the room.

It was a simple room, the wallpaper fading over the years, the left upper corner had started to come off. There was a tear in the middle. She glanced outside the window and saw the side of the mansion. She went downstairs to get the other bags and heard her mother moving inside the kitchen. Once all the bags were carried upstairs, she sank onto the wooden floor not bothering to turn the light on. Why did she not explain more about the journey? She should have asked her mother how she was doing. Or could have simply told her how well she had looked. She should have hugged her back and told her the things on her mind. She regretted coming up to the room instead of continuing with the conversation. Another wave of exhaustion ran through her body.

"I couldn't. Not after being stared at like that," she told herself but she knew well that it was only an excuse. Realising she had not asked about her younger brother, Mei huddled into a corner and closed her eyes. All her practiced speeches had been squandered in a mere five minutes. Heart sinking, nauseated, she yanked her eyes open and reached for her bag. To take her mind off things, she began to unpack. Careful not to disturb her mother, she went down stairs with her laundry, and started the washing machine while she hand washed the others. Picked the dress she wore to the competition, lathered the washing soap gingerly and washed it under warm water. The sound of the clothes against the water in the sink made her more at ease and the nausea ebbed away. She took time and care, hung everything in a neat straight line on the drying pole.

There were only two dinners ready. Mei knew that her younger brother must be away helping on the farm so she decided not to ask about him. The mother and daughter sat quietly at the table, their palms together in front of their chests. Mei murmured a quick prayer while her mother listened and prayed. They ate thin soup with leeks in silence. The rice was mixed with barley to create volume. The daughter swiftly poured some soy sauce into her rice while her mother stood up for a glass of water. The soy sauce did not help. The taste of barley reminded her again that she had come back home. Was she glad that the competition was over, or upset that everything was just as they had been before the journey, she wondered.

She said goodnight to her mother and went up to her room. Upstairs, she sat hands clasped together on top of her old desk, recalling her mother's hand quivering at the mention of the competition. She picked the prize out of her bag and gently placed it in front of another one, eyeing rows of prizes already on her desk. Her last object was by far the most acclaimed and worthy of praise. However, at that moment, it felt empty and not worth looking at, just another glass ornament. She took out a thin blanket from the wardrobe and checked to see the hole in the corner. Feeling the material with her right hand, she stretched it to soothe out the crease. With the hole to guide her, she made sure the blanket was the right way round. She was grateful for the warmth.

In the dark, thoughts came into her mind one after the other. She began to sense all her troubles rushing through, gnawing at her stomach. She commanded herself to think of something positive beginning with the image of her younger brother's jovial face at the gift she had bought for him. He loved trains, especially the old ones. Mei had searched for the perfect present while she was taking the journey, including bookmarks and postcards with all kinds of trains on them. She was particularly pleased with a toy from Germany. It was a small moss green train, the size of a pencil case. She was not sure what kind of metal it was, but it felt very heavy in her hand when she first touched it. Its simplicity and the coldness that spread through her fingers attracted her and she was sure that her brother would like it too.

She wondered what he would say about the competition. Her brother was one of the people who encouraged and helped her convince their mother to let her go. He would be very pleased with the outcome. Her mind drifted to her dead father. What would he say to her? Would he simply give her a warm smile and hug her in his big arms? Or would he play with her long hair and gaze into her eyes like a proud father? Suddenly, the image was taken over by her mother's piercing eyes. Those eyes which conveyed love of a mother to a daughter, but deep down Mei could feel the anger and hatred that she could not understand.

The blanket did not seem to be warm enough any more. She started to massage her arms and move her legs. Forcing herself to think about her father and the train she bought for her brother, she sang melodies in her head but the melody brought back the pressure she had endured through the competition. The rides that made her back ache, the conversations and the arguments she had before the journey. Everything was coming back to her in a single wave enveloping her. Clinging onto the blanket, she strived within her own mind. It was hours before she finally fell asleep.

Next morning Mei woke up with an anxiety, but at least her back pain had gone. Reluctant to face her mother, Mei wondered if she should stay in for the whole morning. She could hear her mother moving about the kitchen, she was preparing for breakfast. The sounds of plates and pans continued for a quarter of an hour. Mei listened as the sound moved to the bathroom. Her mother always tied her hair in a single, neat bun. More faint sounds could be heard from the bathroom. Several minutes later, she heard her mother walk out of the room, into the corridor and shut the door behind her. Mei was annoyed at her own sense of relief at the sound of the door shutting. How could she still be so scared at a person downstairs? Mei gave a big sigh. Ignoring her hunger, she fell asleep again, after adjusting her blanket.

It was past midday when she finally got dressed and ate her breakfast. Mei washed the dishes and noticed a hairbrush next to the cups. She immediately went to the entrance and found her leather shoes newly polished, hurried up stairs, changed into a clean, long skirt, brushed her hair neatly and smiled a weak smile to the mirror. In her room, she sat on her chair. Her hands clasped in a tight grip, staring at the glass ornament. Gingerly, she took it in her hand, but put it back with a sigh. Stood up, sat down again. Her mother would not like it if she had the prize in her hand. Making up her mind to leave it behind, she took only a paper bag and stepped outside.

It was brighter than yesterday. The clouds were moving slowly, revealing the sun now and then. Yet the air felt colder to her. She walked the well-kept path leading to the servants' quarters of the mansion. From this spot she could see the whole front garden with the big apple tree. As a child, she loved picking the apples, and used to bring them into the kitchen. The cook would make sweets with them and serve it at dinner for the residents of the mansion. The cook would always leave just enough for her and other servants' children. She remembered how they loved eating them without their parents knowing. Mei was already at the servants' quarters when she had finished reminiscing about it. She knocked on the door; it had been quite a while since she had last done that.

An old woman welcomed her and she went inside. She asked her how she was and Mei simply gave a timid nod and asked for her mother. The old woman informed her that she was coming in a minute. Mei straightened her back, patted her skirt gently and walked to the corridor. Noticing her daughter, her mother gestured her to come along with her. Walking half a step behind her, she followed her mother. The corridor echoed nothing but their footsteps. Mei watched her mother's back. Her shoulders and neck seemed so frail but yet there was a presence, even an aura that surrounded her thin body that kept people at a distance. The daughter wondered sadly how long it had been since her mother had taken her hand in hand. In the dining room, a well-dressed old couple were finishing their tea. Upon seeing the two, a plump woman walked up to them. Mrs. Kim took Mei by the hand and gave a warm, good-natured smile. Mei smiled back.

"Mei, my dear, I am so glad to see you back. Did you eat your vegetables like you promised?" asked Mrs. Kim while her mother stood silently in the corner of the room.

"Yes I did, madam."

"Mr. Kim, look who's back!" she said to her husband. A short man his belly sticking out, no taller than Mei. In fact, his suit buttons were in danger of falling off.

"You have grown in a year, you look healthy and beautiful as ever, dear child." His eye wrinkles deepening as he smiled and started to ask about the competition, but his wife cut him short by asking when she got back.

"Yesterday, late in the evening, madam," answered Mei, worried how her mother was taking it all, but she could not see with her back facing her. The old couple asked the mother and the daughter to sit down. The mother declined and gestured that she would go back to work, with their permission.

"By all means," said Mrs. Kim. Mei watched her mother go, half relieved that she was leaving.

"So tell me all about the journey!" Mrs. Kim said, "you've been gone almost a whole year, we all missed you!"

Mei thanked the couple for their kind concern and started to talk about her journey. She told them in detail about the long rides she had to endure. She told them about the cities she visited, apologising for not knowing a lot about them since she had spent most of the time practicing in her room. The old mistress nodded understandingly but Mei knowing how Mrs. Kim loved the cities in the western parts of the world, noted her disappointed face. She felt sorry that she was not able to provide them with stories.

"There was the flute player in the café," Mei began, and told them about the incident.

"Did you sing along?" asked Mrs. Kim.

"No, madam, I have no such courage," replied Mei, her eyes downcast.

"You have the courage to play in front of a thousand people in recitals and not in a café," Mrs. Kim laughed and her whole body went up and down. Mr. Kim and Mei joined in and they all laughed merrily.

In the late afternoon, Mei handed the present that she had bought for her master and mistress.

"My master, and madam, thank you for all the encouragement and support you have given me, I am truly grateful for all you have done to me. Please accept these small souvenirs I have found on the journey.

"Mei, you need not have done this," Mrs. Kim told her, "thank you very much child, I never expected, I am so surprised!" She smiled and the chubby cheeks turned rosy. Her cheeks reminded Mei of the childhood days when the mistress had bought sweets to her and her brother.

"Please open it," Mei said timidly but with a smile, "it is not much…"

"Of course it is child, you are too modest," Mrs. Kim opened the case and saw a silver necklace inside.

"What a beautiful necklace, put it on me my dear." Mrs. Kim handed the necklace to Mei and she took it gingerly in her hands. Clumsily she put it around her neck.

"How do I look?" Mrs. Kim turned to Mei and then to her husband.

"It looks very good on you," said Mr. Kim a little too enthusiastically while Mei stifled her laugh.

"Mei, what is it? Is it a monument?" asked Mrs. Kim, feeling the pendant.

"It is a castle in Germany, with many towers."

"Ah, yes, I can feel the towers, Mr. Kim do you see?" Mrs. Kim leaned over to her husband so that he could take a good look at it. This time, Mr. Kim simply nodded good-naturedly.

"Master, here is a present for you, sir."

"Thank you my dear," Mr. Kim accepted his gift and opened it to discover a handsome necktie inside.

"I bought it in a small shop in Italy, I hope you like it, sir."

"Oh, what a beautiful gift, thank you, I shall wear it the next time I go to town." Mr. Kim shook Mei's hand. She turned crimson but was glad that both liked the presents.

"Ah, look at the time! I think you better get home, I don't want you to catch a cold with the evening wind, we can continue our conversation another day."

Mei thanked them again while Mrs. Kim fussed over catching a cold. The old couple smiled again as she left the room. She felt a surge of warmth filling her stomach. Having grandparents must be just like that, she thought as she walked down the path.

YOUR BIRDS AND YOUR FISH

Erika Martin

Deep inside the dark, dark blue of my night
your finger blossomed like a rose.
Letting go
in spasms and ribbons
till your birds and your fish
flooded within
all feathers and fins
heaving
straining
inside.
They tickled, I laughed
then cried as your arms
locked me up
in your love.

TIGER MOTH

Graham Joyce

Lenny suspected that other lawyers were passing him mad clients. He was known around town for his soft-shell, and neither the competition nor his own firm were above abusing his good nature. Not that he hadn't passed over a funny-farm client or a litigious bore himself. That was in the mix; everybody did it if the file got too long or if they were getting through too many cans of air-freshener after taking an affidavit. But fair is fair and bad law had to be spread around evenly.

Lenny was a matrimonial solicitor in the Norfolk seaside town of Hunstanton. He occupied an office cluttered with files, framed photographs and obsolete law books belonging to a senior partner who himself occupied a minimalist, dust-free suite across the hall. Plucking up his gold-nibbed ink fountain pen, a theatrical prop he kept to impress the likes of his present client, Lenny put the question.

"Mrs Grapes, why you do think the man you are living with is not your husband?"

"I already told you. He was very thin when we got married. Slim as a cigarette. I don't know what happened to my real husband. I don't know where this man came from." Mrs Grapes dabbed her eyes with the tissue Lenny had given her.

"And when did this fatness occur?"

Mrs Grapes blinked at the question. In truth, Lenny did too. He couldn't remember when in the last dozen years of legal practice he had phrased such a bad question. The fact is he wasn't paying proper attention. He was trying to remember which of his legal 'friends' had steered him the case.

Mrs Grapes, herself thin to the point of a disturbingly translucent skin, shifted on her bony haunches and tried to frame a reply.

"Mrs Grapes," Lenny said, making it easier for her, "are you absolutely certain that this man is not your husband?"

"I told you already. I married a thin man, not this huge fat person. I want a divorce."

Lenny looked at the door, the window, the small ventilator panel in the upper corner of the room: all the usual means of egress. As Mrs Grapes outlined her suspicions further, he fought a noisy internal dialogue about how he might tactfully get her out of the room, legally and with kindness.

Whenever Lenny found himself in a legal grey area, a point at which the meaning of the law might have to be massaged, he had a give-away habit of shaping his mouth into an O before speaking.

"Mrs Grapes, if this man is masquerading as your husband then it's a criminal matter, not a civil one."

"Oh?"

"That's correct, Mrs Grapes. I have to advise you on a point of law that you can't divorce this man because you never married him."

"Oh?"

Lenny got out of his seat and came round the table. "Indeed. You can't go around divorcing people you never married in the first place. And you do after all seem certain he's not the man you married. Mrs Grapes, what you need is the police. Who will be vigorous in their efforts to help you."

He was already gently raising Mrs Grapes by her elbow out of her chair and leading her to the anteroom to his office. There the secretary Lenny shared with the firm's senior partner tried to slip a gardening magazine onto her knees. She was known as 'the redoubtable Susan', an epithet that baffled Lenny.

"Susan, could you look after my client? Mrs Grapes, my secretary here will give you the number of the police station."

"I will," Susan said, "but I'm very stressed."

Mrs Grapes, impressed that her case warranted immediate police attention rather than the lumbering machinery of the law, seemed grateful and happy to leave. Lenny closed his office door, sank back in his seat and pulled off his tie.

Moments later Susan walked in without knocking and dumped a pile of new files on his desk.

"What's this?" he asked.

"Mr Falconer is hard pressed and wanted you to take these extra cases on. You're lucky I brought them. I shouldn't be carrying all of these things, what with my back."

"No, Susan."

After she had left, Lenny made a call.

"Simon, is that job in Nottingham still available?"

Simon had studied law with Lenny at Nottingham Trent University. Lenny was best man at his wedding. Simon's wife Elizabeth was always trying to fix Lenny up romantically. Beautiful, kind Elizabeth, on whom Lenny secretly doted, didn't think a thirty-five year old man should still be living with his mother and told him so, often.

"I spoke to George only yesterday. Said he's very keen to see you."

"Know what? I've been in this town too long."

"They dump on you Lenny. What happened now?"

"Nothing. Just don't let Elizabeth see your fat-rolls."

After talking to Simon, Lenny put a call through to the Nottingham legal firm of Chortleman & Brace, to arrange an informal lunch date for the following day. Then he asked the redoubtable Susan to re-arrange all his morning appointments.

Susan made an unnecessary venting noise. "I will but I'm very stressed." Susan shopped at the same stores as Lenny's mother. She wore long kilts and lacy blouses, and kept a tiny tissue tucked inside her sleeve. Hauling herself out of her typing chair, she made her kilt swing aggressively as she stepped over to the filing cabinet. The cabinet drawer was rattled opened and banged shut. The relevant files thwacked her desk. "Very stressed."

"Yes," said Lenny. "I can see that."

Mrs Grapes was Lenny's last client of the day. He gathered up the burden of the new files to take home and slipped out of the back door, trying to be discreet as he shuffled across the car park to his Saab. He sat behind the wheel for a moment wondering how he might break the news to his mother that he was considering a job in Nottingham.

"Well, you know best," his mother said.

She'd just served up a familiar dinner of steamed haddock, mashed potatoes and peas. Lenny looked through the steam rising from the fish, saw his mother compress her lips, and regretted blurting out his news. His stomach squeezed. He knew he wouldn't be able to eat one forkful of the meal before him. The worst of all possible responses was to hear his Mother say that he, Lenny, knew best. When Lenny knew best, his mother often set her features and said not a single word for several days.

"It's just a preliminary discussion. An exploration. They probably won't even offer me the job."

His mother said nothing to that, hacking at her fish as if it were tough steak.

Lenny and his mother had relocated to the coastal town of Hunstanton shortly after his father had died of an unexpected aneurysm when Lenny was nine years old. His mother couldn't face the old house. It reminded her too much of the husband she'd lost. In fact she hadn't coped too well with the new life either, and Lenny soon became the man of the house, with an emotionally dependent mother. Lenny had missed the opportunity to escape through studying for a law degree. He made the fatal mistake of moving back in with his mother when he was offered a job in his home town. Several years on Mrs Pearce still baked and iced cup cakes and sprinkled them with hundreds-and-thousands every Sunday afternoon. Lenny's favourites, she said. She made his cocoa every night at nine-thirty in the evening. Lenny's routine. She washed and pressed all of his clothes for him, and she even pressed his socks. Lenny's preference.

When Lenny had first mentioned the idea of Nottingham, his mother had laid down the fish slice and said, "But think of the commuting time! You'd have to drive right around The Wash and then across the country. All of those winding roads!"

"Well I'd stay in Nottingham," Lenny had said. Then, too late and unable to save himself, as he saw her stiffen he'd added. "Except for week-ends."

Lenny pushed his food around on his plate before retiring to his room. Not fond of the lace frills and cotton flounces and ubiquitous glass ornaments favoured by his mother, he often beat a retreat to the sanctuary of his bedroom. There he lay on his bed, hands folded behind his head, staring up at the model aeroplanes suspended from the ceiling by invisible lengths of cotton.

But Lenny knew best. And while even the sweetest but somewhat possessive mother might say, *right then, wash and press your own stinky socks buster, and your shirt and trousers too,* Lenny's mother rose in the morning, still marbled in silence, and laid out his shirt and tie, polished his shoes til they gleamed and brushed down his best dark suit.

"It's not an interview Mum, it's a chat. My jacket will be more comfortable."

"You know best, Leonard." She hung the suit back in his wardrobe, took down the jacket and began to brush it for lint with stiff, downward strokes. Then she held it for him to slip into.

"I'll be back mid-afternoon, Mum."

"As you wish."

Mrs Pearce opened the door for her son but failed to offer her cheek for the ritual peck. He kissed her anyway and hurried to his Saab. Lenny glanced back before he drove away. His mother, motionless, watched from the window.

His mother was entirely correct about the drive to Nottingham. It was necessary to hug the coastal rode to King's Lynn, through the flat reclaimed land around The Wash before cutting across fen land on the way over to Nottingham. It was a winding drive alongside grassy dikes and irrigation ditches, past muddy reed-beds and canals teeming with eels under the open sky of Lincolnshire; a wind-blasted land reeking of brine. It was a land much beloved by Lenny, but which had one day mysteriously become his prison.

At a service station he stopped to fill up the tank, loitering, already early for his appointment. In the washroom he looked hard at his gentle, slightly pudgy features, wondering if he could slim himself down to a completely different person, one who might replace a woman's husband or a mother's son. His hand strayed to the red-and-yellow metal badge pinned to his lapel. He considered removing it, wondering if it made him look childish. But he left it. The badge was, after all, talismanic. It was a badge of a De Havilland Tiger Moth biplane. He'd found it in the grass shortly after he'd moved to the area with his mother almost twenty-five years earlier, on what had been a momentous day.

It was shortly after his father had died and the first time he and his mother had ventured out of their new home together. He'd had to beg her to take him out of a house rattling with his father's ghost, even though his father had never lived there. His mother had trailed the ghost all the way to Hunstanton. She never let a day go by without referring to his father or without making him the standard by which Lenny should measure his life.

Then Lenny hit upon the expedient of saying, "Dad would have liked it." He was learning to fight ghosts with ghosts. So his mother, dragging chains she'd made for herself, had made a brief, nervous drive to the beach. There she sat in a deck chair, knees pressed together, sweltering in a woollen cardigan. She'd made Lenny swear he wouldn't stray to far from the beach, already exhibiting a terror of being left alone out of doors, even for an hour.

But Lenny had of course strayed behind the beach and over the dunes to the coastal road. On the other side of the road was a steep grassy dike, and on the dike two boys were beating tremendous fun out of a giant cardboard box. The boys carried the box to the crest of the dike, climbed inside it and then powered themselves down the slope. In a pitch of raucous laughter they were spilled into the dry gully at the foot of the dike before dragging the box back up the gradient and repeating the ride. The boys, both about his own age, made it seem the most uproarious fun a boy could have in the world, and in watching them Lenny felt the deep sting of loneliness.

He ventured across the road.

With another ride imminent one of the boys shouted from the top of the hill. "There's another Willard, Willard."

"Aye Willard," said the smaller of the boys. "Looks to me like a Willard, Willard."

"Come aboard Willard!" shouted the first boy. He beckoned Lenny on.

Lenny looked behind him for someone who might be called Willard. The dunes were utterly deserted, and the road was clear. The sun baked down, and seemed to move a notch in the sky, as if operated on a ratchet. Lenny squinted back at the boys, whose white shirts flared in the brilliant sunlight.

"Yes, you Willard!" said the first boy. "Come aboard! We're about to let her rip!"

"Look sharp Willard," said his companion. "You don't want to miss this!"

Lenny glanced behind him again, stupidly. There was no one there. The two boys were indeed talking to him, gazing down at him, expectant, as if his decision to join them were momentous. Lenny began climbing the steep grassy bank.

"Hurrah, Willard's joining us!"

"Good chap Willard, climb aboard, plenty of room!"

Lenny panted at the top of the slope. "My name isn't Willard."

The first boy, older with sleek black hair and liquid dark eyes shouted, "He says his name isn't Willard, Willard."

"Of course it's Willard, Willard." His pal had a wild tousle of brown hair and a face full of freckles. "Jump in Willard. There's a chap."

Lenny got in anyway. It was a squeeze, but he saw that he could slide his legs around the boy in front.

"Willard's maiden flight!" yelled the dark-haired boy. "Fuel levels?"

"Check," his friend returned.

"Altimeter?"

"Check"

"Confubulator?"

"Check."

"Chocks away!"

They pushed off. The box slipped easily down the slope, propelled by the weight of the three boys. It gathered speed as it went, then as it hit the gully at the bottom it pitched the three boys right out of the box into a clattering, giggling heap.

"All okay Willard 2?" shouted the slightly older boy.

"Okay," replied the freckled lad.

"Okay Willard 3?" He stared hard at Lenny.

"Okay."

"Good! Then once more to the breach!"

Everything about the boys' behaviour and speech was puzzling, but was compensated for by the scale of hysterical fun afforded by the brief ride in the cardboard box. Even if their phrases belonged to a forgotten time, the warmth and friendly overtures exhibited by the boys was startling in contrast to the usual surliness and hostility common to most boys of that age.

"The new Willard is a good egg, Willard."

"Jolly good egg Willard."

"My name's not Willard, it's Lenny."

The older boy stopped in his tracks. He set down the box, put an arm round Lenny's shoulder and spoke confidentially.

"Look, it's a crashing bore isn't it, when you come on holiday, to learn another chap's name. Far easier if everyone is called Willard. I'm Willard 1, my brother is Willard 2, you're Willard 3. Right Willard?"

Lenny met the boy's swimming dark eyes full on. "Understood, Willard."

"The new Willard catches on fast, Willard."

"Three cheers for the new Willard!"

And after cheers, the cardboard box runs went on and on, and if the baking sun slipped a further notch in the sky none of the boys noticed. The box runs went on until disaster struck, when Willard 1 noticed the loss of a pin-badge.

"It must have come off in the grass."

"What's it look like?" Lenny asked.

"It's a biplane. We're going to be fighter pilots when we're grown up. Isn't that right Willard?"

"Right Willard."

Lenny wasn't sure what a biplane was but didn't like to ask. As for fighter pilots, his only notion of a career was that his mother had told him he was going to be a doctor or a lawyer. In any event, together the three of them combed the grass without success. And in that time the shadow of the dike crept longer.

Willard 1 seemed especially depressed at losing his pin-badge, but hunting for it was a lost cause. The search was interrupted when there came the sound of an engine in the sky, approaching from seaward. The three boys looked up. It was an old-fashioned biplane flying low, chugging over their heads, its engine popping, low enough to see the pilot in his leathers.

Tiger Moth

"It's a De Havilland!" shouted Willard 1, as if astonished. "What a stroke of luck!"

"A Tiger Moth!" shrieked Willard 2, barely able to contain his excitement.

Lenny, to whom these words meant nothing, shielded his eyes from the sun and looked up at the double-winged craft soaring overhead.

"But that must be a sign!" shouted Willard 2 to his brother. "Don't you see? You just lost a Tiger Moth pin-badge, and then one flies right overhead! It's a sign!"

"By God you're right Willard!" He turned and watched the biplane chug away from them, trailing clouds of vapour. "We have to follow it!"

The boys ran up over the dike and set off in pursuit of the biplane.

"Come on Willard 3!" one of them called without looking back.

Lenny followed an instinct to scramble up the dike after the boys. He saw them chasing across the flat, reedy land as the plane banked and flew off in the direction of the sun. But Lenny faltered, remembering his mother sitting on the beach. He hesitated on the crest of the dike as the biplane disappeared across the horizon. Lenny heard the boys calling as they ran, saw them scramble up a second dike until they too disappeared behind it.

Lenny waited in an ecstasy of indecision. Too late he decided to go after the boys, but when he reached the crest of the second dike he'd lost sight of them. They were nowhere in the vista before him.

He trudged back to the place where the cardboard box lay abandoned. The sun had become a burnished coin in the sky and the shadows were long. Lenny tried taking a solo ride down the dike, but now the cardboard box was somehow discharged of all its joy. He felt as though he had missed an opportunity among the lords of life; that he'd allowed his mother to chain him back; that he should have gone when they called, wherever they went and whatever the consequences. Moreover the boys had taken with them the wings of the afternoon and Lenny was left to stand in the cool, creeping shadow of the dike.

But as he put down the box, Lenny found in the grass the lost pin-badge. He held it up to the sunlight, like an offering, and kept it as a souvenir in the hope he might one day encounter the boys again. This memento of the afternoon almost compensated for the reception with which his mother greeted him when he returned to the beach.

She turned on him a white-cold fury. "Where have you been?"

"Playing."

"Playing? And didn't it occur to you that I would be sickened and worried senseless while you were playing? And what with your father only dead a few weeks? Didn't it occur to you that I might think you yourself were dead? Didn't it? Didn't it occur to you that I was left here alone? Haven't you anything but selfishness in your heart Leonard? And your father dead just a few weeks and me alone on the beach! Your father would be ashamed of you. Ashamed. He would never, ever, ever leave me alone like that. Never."

"I'm sorry."

But she'd said her piece. And with that she turned on him a silence that had persisted for several days, and it was a punishment that had lasted Lenny a lifetime. It was a pattern repeated when he'd tried to bring girlfriends into his life, or when he'd tried to take a holiday without her. The ghost of his dead father, ashamed at his nine-year-old son's selfishness, never had to be invoked again.

The informal interview went well for Lenny. Chortleman of Chortleman & Brace had retired and George Brace was shaking lose a few cobwebs. He made it easy for Lenny.

"What fees are you earning over there Lenny?"

Lenny told him. Brace blinked. "Substantial caseload?"

Lenny described a caseload that some might call backbreaking. Brace blinked again.

"And what are they paying you?"

Lenny told him. Brace blinked a third time and said, "Hell, Lenny, we'll knock that into a cocked hat."

"Serious?"

"I'm sorry to say this but they're laughing at you. We can up that figure by twenty five per cent, plus we've got health and pension plans we stitched in ourselves. I'll be straight: we need you to run matrimonial. Divorce is booming and yet marriage is still fashionable. Every one's a winner for us. Plus summer holidays will be over soon and the caseloads rocket after all that hideous togetherness, you know that. We want you Lenny. Say yes."

"Gosh. I really don't know. I'd have to uproot. It's a lot of fuss."

"Generous re-location package. Full secretarial support. Everything, Lenny."

Lenny promised he'd give it serious thought, and George Brace drove him out to The Millwheel for lunch, where they parked amid the Jags and the Mercs. Over roast duckling and asparagus tips Lenny told George about Mrs Grapes, whose thin husband had been usurped by a fat husband, and George laughed all over the place.

"That's a funny story," George said.
"Sad, too."
"Yes," George agreed. "Sad too."

Lenny took his time over the drive home. He told himself he wanted to suck in the country air but really he was avoiding having to face his mother. He wanted this job like a bird wants the air but he knew he wouldn't take it. It wasn't the first informal interview he'd been to over the years. He just wouldn't be able to look his mother in the eye and tell her that he was leaving her.

As he drove through the waterlands around the fens the sun began to dip, dispatching shadows from the canals and the dikes. He opened his car window to inhale some of the odour of the baked earth and the muddy silt commingled and he decided it was a good smell. Then as he took the coastal road towards Hunstanton he looked across at a steep dike and what he saw made him stop the car and get out.

Two lads cavorted with a cardboard box on the crest of the dike, with the sun dipping behind them. Silhouetted, they played in the exact spot where he'd encountered those other boys almost a quarter-century earlier. Lenny couldn't repress a laugh of recognition.

He made his way over as they came shooting down the dike in the cardboard box, spilling into the gully in gales of laughter. But when he drew up close, the smile disappeared from his lips. One of the lads had sleek black hair and liquid brown eyes. The other had a tousled brown mop and a face full of freckles. They were sprawled now in the shadow of the dike, suddenly aware of him.

"Boys," Lenny said. "Boys." He was standing in strong sunlight, beyond the reach of the dike shadow. He had to shield his eyes from the low sun.

"What?" one of them asked. "What is it?"

But Lenny couldn't speak. It was too absurd. What could he say? He continued to peer at them from beneath the flat visor of his hand. The boys stepped out of the shadow and into the light. Yet even though he was now but a few steps from them, and though they stood in the full glare of the sun, the boys' features remained disguised in half-silhouette. They were the colour of grey slate. A wave of revulsion passed through him.

Then the expression on the boys' faces changed. They looked at him in an ugly manner, suspicious, as if they thought he meant to harm them in some way.

"Look Willard," said the younger of the two. "He's got your pin-badge."

The older boy got to his feet, his face still dark, squinting at the badge on Lenny's lapel. "You're right Willard, how come he's he got my badge?"

"Willard!" Lenny shouted, fumbling now with the pin-badge, trying to remove it so as to hand it back. "That's it! I remember! Willard!"

"He must be a thief, Willard," said the younger boy. "He must have stolen it!"

"No no no!" Lenny protested. "I found it! Right here in the grass! I never stole it!"

The older boy eyed the badge proffered by Lenny. Then he turned and began scrambling up the dike. "Let's get out of here Willard!"

The second boy followed up the dike. "That's right Willard. We don't want to hang around amongst thieves."

Lenny raced after them. "Wait! I didn't steal it! I want to return it. I've had it all this time!" But his shoes slipped on the grassy bank and his knee collided with the turf and twisted. As he got to his feet, Lenny looked back at the road. A car had slowed down to see what he was doing. He knew he must look ridiculous, a grown man scrambling after two boys.

But he went anyway, and when he got to the top of the gradient he could see the boys already disappearing over the second dike. He followed, and just as before, by the time he'd climbed the second dike the boys were nowhere to be seen in the flat, marshy expanse before him. As the sun dipped behind trees the landscape was plunged into shadow, and the temperature dropped palpably. And though Lenny's heart was bursting to follow the boys, some other instinct, some life-preserving reflex told him that he mustn't. But as he gazed across the shadowy marshland, with the yellow sun winking behind the charcoal sketch of trees in the distant wood, he heard a piercing, bird-like cry of sorrow.

Back in his car, Lenny sat behind the wheel for some time. An hour passed before, with trembling fingers, he re-fixed the pin-badge to his lapel, started the ignition and drove home.

"You're later than I expected," his mother said.

"Yes; it went on."

"I thought something had happened to you on the road. I was worried."

"No. I'm fine and dandy."

She served up dinner. It was cottage pie, carrots and peas, steam billowing upward as she removed it from the hot oven. "I managed to keep this warm. And I've made some gravy."

He peered through the thin cloud coming off the dish, wondering how many dinners of steamed fish and cottage pie he would be made to consume. "Lovely Mother. It looks lovely."

He ate without pleasure, and after he was done he put his knife and fork together neatly on his plate and said in a quiet, firm voice.

"I got offered a job in Nottingham. A very good job. I've decided to take it."

She stood up without a word and made to take his plate away, but Lenny said, "No Mum, you sit down, while I tell you about this. You sit down."

She sat and compressed her lips while he looked her in the eye and told her all about the benefits of the job, about Chortleman & Brace, about his plans and about how often he planned to visit her after he'd made the move.

"You know best," was all she would say.

"Yes," Lenny said. "I do. I really do."

Later he went and laid down on his bed, with his hands behind his head, gazing up at the model aeroplanes suspended from the ceiling. He knew that the boys had given him a second chance to follow them. Not into the shade, nor into the mudflats stolen from the sea, not into a land of silhouette, no, none of those dark valleys. But somewhere for himself, where he might make his own way.

He thought of his future in Nottingham. He thought of the pin-badge; and of the Tiger Moth biplane; and of where the cavorting boys play forever on the crest of the grassy dike and in its creeping shadow.

SLEEPING BEAUTY

Roberta J Dewa

He met the married couple in the village pub, not long after his divorce had come through, and the world he found himself in was still soft enough to take new impressions. They remembered his face from a series of classic roles he had played on TV during the seventies: Ariel, Chéri, Demetrius, but they remembered different things. The husband talked quotations and productions until his words yellowed and dropped like a stain on the objects around them; the wife kept her head down and her voice muted until, at last, she raised her head and looked at the actor and said:

"You wore a lilac shirt when you played Chéri. I remember all the colours, but the lilac best of all. You have to be very dark to wear lilac."

The husband gave an embarrassed laugh and squeezed her hand, but the actor was flattered and revived in a breathless way that was strange to him, and he stayed with them for the rest of the evening, while Steven's monologue drifted like smoke around them. He watched the shifts in her gaze, her dull eyes fixed on the huddles around the bar and on the gleam of brass and brown tilted liquid; he watched her sudden bright eyes, when they fastened on the hair he kept longer than was fashionable, the hair he kept dark at heavier expense. By the time they had all given hands and names, he had her invitation in his hand and Steven's directions in his head; and he said, "See you next Saturday, then," and turned his back and made his exit slowly, with the feel of her hands in his hair like a slow stroking ripple of applause.

And outside, in the dark night air, when he thought of their stillness as a couple: his by his own design, hers by someone else's, the vigour flowed in him as years ago, when he had taken on a new role.

What he could see of the house rising up on the billow of its surrounding wilderness looked *fin de siécle*; he thought he glimpsed the edges of crenellations and turrets, or perhaps only ornate and fantastically tiled chimneypots; the garden facing him through the spiked iron uprights of the gates destroyed all sense of scale. He spoke into the grille beside them that spat static back into his face and heard her whisper "Hi," and said, "It's Paul. We met -" and one of the gates moved inward, surprisingly silent, before he had finished. Beyond the sweep the drive became grassy, shaded first by trees and then brambles, tough stems mounding on their layers of dead and fruiting wood and prospecting outward with virulent green suckers. As he contoured around them he caught metallic glints far back in the piled gloom. What looked like a watch hung from a twig; a thin chain twined two leaves together; closer to the drive scraps of fabric flickered in the branches, handkerchiefs or knotted flags with their colours fading. He found himself thinking of eastern religions, of souls fluttering in mountains where the air was stretched too thin; he thought he was in Poe, or Stoker, or du Maurier at least, but it was the first guess that clung to him as he bent to free his ankle from the branch that trailed and tugged at it and finally released him whiplike, with a lashing rebound.

Then he saw the scratches on the backs of his hands. And the Gothic door, with her standing outside it, wearing a long green dress.

"I'm sorry," she said in her faintest voice. "Most people bring their cars round the back."

"I'm banned," he said, "I got a lift. I'll wash it off, it doesn't matter."

"Of course it does," she said, frowning at the red on flesh-tone. "For you, it matters."

He saw Steven miming and beckoning from a window. She turned and touched his hand and the touch was not a hint, but a part of an action, yet to be completed.

"He's explaining to his friends how you came the wrong way. He'll make a joke of it, a kind of parable. He makes a joke of everything."

He followed her into the light and the pockets of noise and laughter and curious, incurious glances. Steven greeted him loudly and propelled him into groups with the dead weight of a hand upon his shoulder and introduced him as "our classical actor friend. See if you can get him to tell you what he's doing now." The men quickly lost interest in his account of provincial theatres and Shakespearian readings, while the women recognized him in a flash of excitement that passed mindlessly through their numbers like a Mexican wave. They moved in a circle around him, scanning his face for signs of corporeal decay, for the slow fall of flesh from cheeks exposed in profile, the bottle-sheen of the hair she had wanted to touch. He skimmed every encounter and held his hands up for excuse and then looked for her in corners and landings until he found her in a child's pose on the topmost stair with her arms around the carved rose finial of the banister. She dropped her head and smiled and he joined her.

"Your husband tried to revive the corpse of my old triumphs and his friends looked for new ones. They failed, so I've escaped."

"Good," she said, "Good. Now we have to see to your hands."

He looked at them. The streaks were dry. Her touching them would make them wet and stinging once again. Her touch would be soft, it would smell of old-fashioned balm. It would be a continuation of the action.

"Come and see my bathroom," she said.

The colour scheme in the fragrant room was green and lilac. He washed his hands in lavender soap and looked at the bottles and compacts and tubes arranged on a shelf that ran almost round the room, displayed so that the word that appeared on every label faced outward. He scanned the shelf more than once, in case there was a rogue product without it; but she was consistent.

"This is my beauty circle," she said, dripping water very gently over the backs of his hands, "it keeps the ugliness outside at bay. But it's just a word, until it is embodied." She looked nervously and defiantly at him. He could hardly hear her voice. "You embody the word. You're beautiful."

He followed her down the corridor like a drunk wrapped inside and out in fog; exhilarated, oblivious of harm.

She opened the second door and the room stretched out before him, high and spacious, like a gallery. The larger room also smelt of lavender, unless he had brought the scent in with him. It was dimly lit; the light was spot-light, each arc hung over a dark-framed print, and prints enough to cover every wall; typical Victorian subjects, richly coloured pictures of trysts in forests, abbey ruins, country chapel porches, women on pedestals and men on their knees. A woman sprang out of blossom to entwine a naked youth, a woman perched on a rock with a dark desperate man in the water beneath her; a young aristocrat lay cold, his dark head hanging backward, his white shirt open and his white chest catching the light from the half-open window. She was the guide, but with the siren's hair and distant gaze, circling her gallery with her hand trailing until he touched her fingers, and another part of the action fell into place.

She turned slowly, dropping his hand and finding it again, bringing her gaze back to him, letting it rest there.

"I looked for you here after we met last week but I didn't find you. You made the faces look different, somehow; I don't like them as much as I did."

He found the edge of a sofa nest-lined with shawls and pulled her gently down into it. Her body dropped graceful, slow-motion, against him, her eyes considered the circled naked youth opposite them on the wall. She read out the legend inked in Celtic script around the border.

"What I mean by a picture is a beautiful romantic dream of something that never was, and never will be." She twisted round and looked at him; and there was something sudden as he returned the look, a tremor in his view of her. "He should have said the world is ugly, and I hate it. I've said that, seen it many times. Only you came out of it, and now I'm not so sure."

"I'm sure," he said, putting his fragrant hands behind her head. "You want something real."

He kissed her and pulled her lips into a yawn and laid his cool tongue over hers and left it there for a minute so that they were like sleepers together. She slid slowly down the sofa with a lovebird shawl behind her head and the green dress slipping up her body and he saw with a second tremor that she was naked underneath. She parted softly, each flesh-layer sinking inward for him like a pressed rose, yet not too easily, so that the third tremor only came when it was over and she hugged him to her and rolled them both until she sat astride him and pulled the dress-folds from round her neck and flung them away from her, into the gloom.

"Again," she said.

He had a brief, faint echo of the sensation that sometimes came to him when he realized, all at once, that he was very drunk; then he looked at her, and saw the husband's stillness broken out of her; and smiled, and did as he was told.

"You must always wear it like this," she said, "just this length."

Her hands were in his hair, combing and pulling the thick fringe down over the lines on his forehead. Her damp fingers smoothed out the shape of his eyebrows, her fingernail traced a pencil-line beneath his eyes, flicked the lashes and wondered at their length; her free hand cupped his chin and pushed upward, tightening the flesh around his neck. Then she bent and kissed him three times: lips on lip, lips on lip, lips and tongue to make a drawn Cupid's bow of him.

And then he had the fourth tremor, right through his body.

"I have to go to the bathroom," he said. "I need to get a drink."

"Don't be long," she said, watching while he looked for his jeans. "Remember the ugliness out there."

The landing light hurt his eyes after the gloom and the door was locked and as he put his ear to the wood he heard the shuffling of movement inside. He breathed rapidly, stepped away and looked back toward her door. Then the bolt clicked and Steven emerged with a glass in his hand; stopped, and looked at him.

"Hello, Paul," he said. "Having a good time?"

He tried to get past, but Steven stood his ground.

"I hope you're good," he said. "She likes them pretty, but they aren't always good. There's a long word for her condition, too many syllables for me to remember. It's not a word she likes, but a washed-up actor with no ties just fits her bill. She can't go out much, so we bring the entertainment in."

He burst out laughing and shook his head and swayed against the doorframe. His nose and cheeks and his head under its stubble-cut were red from party wine, his blue eyes gleamed with the first expected pleasure of the evening; his top lip lifted, isolated from the other, sufficient for a sneer. Paul stood still and watched and heard her faint voice calling through the door at his back. Then he said only:

"She was right about the world."

The laugh rumbled from deep down, cutting through her voice.

"And you're a bit long in the tooth for Chéri. But she'll never notice in the dark."

He roared again as Paul pushed past him and into the bathroom and slammed the green door. The incantation of her beauty circle bounced its mantra off the mirror and he bent over the basin and retched until his head throbbed with the smell and only the scent on his hands, held up in front of his streaming face, gave him any relief.

"I thought you weren't coming back," she said.

He came into the room and went up to the window and opened it. The horizon of the bramble-patch curved dark against the summer sky, the objects hanging from the branches twinkling like stars. Nothing moved. He could hear the clarity of party goodbyes and the slam of car-doors and shot-bursts of laughter drifting from the other side of the world.

"I thought I wasn't. Then I thought of something."

She got up from the sofa and he saw how gracefully she cried.

"You see I waited for you. And I have been waiting for you, Paul. All my life."

He shut the window and stood against it, his veined hands laid gracefully on the sill.

"I'm taking you away," he said. "No evil husband, no galleries of men, no barbed horizon. Just you and me and happiness."

She twined her arms around him and he felt her hands, deep and deeper in his hair.

"In the morning," she said.

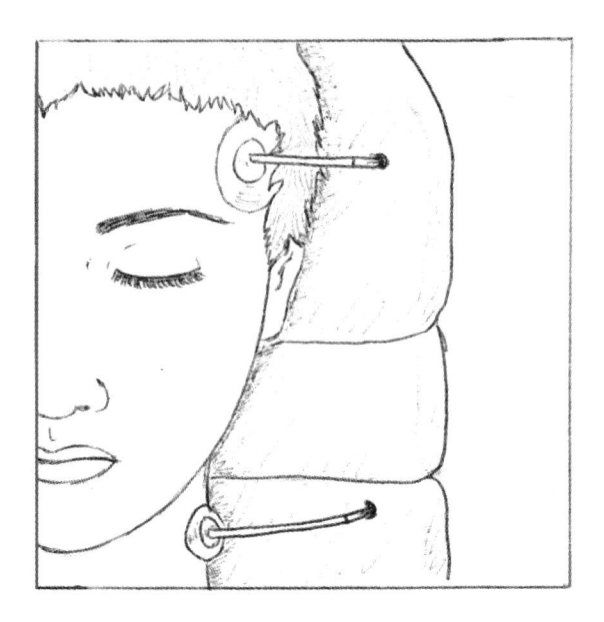

THE REAL THING

Lynda Blagg

My fist slams into Petey's jaw. He doesn't see it coming, drops his pot of Instafood. I follow up with a blow to his guts, an elbow to the nose and as he crouches, holding his face, stomp down hard on his right kneecap. The cartilage shatters and he screams in pain. I clamp a hand over his mouth and laugh as he tries to bite me.

Don't feel sorry for Petey. He asked for this. And anyway, he always, always gets back up.

Every day I come home from work and there's a different stranger bent over the bathtub. I nod in their direction and they mumble a greeting, incoherent because their head's hanging upside down. Then Petey looks up too, fixes me with that insolent turquoise glare and returns to what he's doing. What he's doing is injecting pigment into the client's scalp with painstaking care. Today the dye in the colour gun is purple. Sometimes it's green, or yellow, or blue. Petey can get any colour.

When he's done, the client will have their new vibrant hair colour for six to eight weeks.

I throw my bag onto the kitchen table and it clatters into a pile of Petey's dirty plates. Petey doesn't do dishes. The smell of stale food follows me into my room, which overlooks the yard behind the flat. My room is small and dark. Along the wall my 'Employee of the Month' awards from Premier A are spaced at ten centimetre intervals. There are six, one for every month I've worked at the company. I am always the first one at work in the morning and the last one to leave at night. I take every overtime slot on offer.

I owe it all to Petey.

Premier A is the world's largest and best creator, distributor and host of virtual gaming. I work in the Legal Department, making sure we have the customers' retinal scans and ID prints on file. This acts as proof of their consent to be subjected to a form of electric shock therapy. As with all VR, punters are wired up to our neural network and the game is downloaded directly into their brain. Transmitter pads are slapped on all over their bodies, so they feel every aspect of game play. In a flight simulator, the pads stimulate the right places at the right times, so in the pit of your stomach, you can feel that you're soaring. But you aren't.

The secret of Premier A's success is its willingness to cater for everyone. All the other big firms concentrate on the standard VR fare, the bread and butter of the diehard gamers; fighting, shooting, and flying sims. Premier A has something for everyone. Historical romances, fantasy role-plays, interactive puzzles, even pornography. On a Wednesday night, porn's half price. Lance and I sit on the tills and play spot the pervert. You'd be amazed the people who come out of the woodwork for a cheap thrill.

Lance is the coolest manager ever. A huge man-child with dark cow eyes and a loveable grin. He has little interest in management, but a true passion for his product. Premier A's product. Our product.

I am distracted from admiring my trophies by a slow rhythmic thudding against my window. I draw back the curtain. A couple are having sex; a tall black man perched on my windowsill, straddled by a small white woman. I bang on the raised steel shutter and they start and stumble away, pulling at their clothes. The woman mouths obscenities through the plate glass and I yell a few comments back, knowing they won't make it through the bulletproof coating.

There is a reason our ground floor flat is the cheapest in the complex. As well as being a hook-up hotspot, it is also easily accessible to thieves. We don't have anything of value, but then the people of Red Ford will steal anything. I once caught a guy, drugged up to the eyeballs and jittery as a whippet, loading his pockets with chicken bones and lumps of congealed gravy from our rubbish disposal hatch. When I stared him down, he said; "Sorry man, just hungry," and crawled back under the chain link fence, out into the street.

Man. Everyone calls me man. I guess short hair, flat chest and steel-toecapped boots tick enough boxes. Petey gets just the opposite. Implants have made his cheekbones high. Surgical sculpting means his chin is small and delicately cleft. Lens grafts resulted in those aqua eyes. Add to that his reedy voice and girlish laugh and it's no wonder callers to the flat assume that *I'm* Peter Lazarus and *he's* Maxine French.

No matter how I time it, when I venture out to cook some time later, Petey will be by the microwave, heating packs of instant mush. Petey eats the cheapest, most revolting gunk, just to free up more capital for his body alterations. I asked him once why he didn't just use his money on decent food and the odd trip to the gym. He replied, with a condescending sneer: "No one *waits* for their body to change any more Max. They want to see improvement instantly."

Personally, I wouldn't call what Petey's doing to himself improvement, but evidently there are many who'd disagree. The guy charges two hundred New Euros just to repigment someone's hair. That's expensive, even in the city.

Petey also does black market body alterations. Only small, surface cosmetic stuff, no skeletal work or deep muscular sculpting, but it's still dangerous. On more than one occasion I've had to clean strips of discarded skin out of the bathroom sink when a hydrochloric face peel has gone too deep. Yet people come from all over to do business with him. I don't see the attraction, myself.

And why does Petey do all this? So that when *he* has treatments, he can afford major, state-recognised practitioners with clean, safe surgeries and trained anaesthetists.

Two hundred for hair, more for the shadier stuff, and still he's always broke. He owes me two months' rent. Our comm system got shut down because he ran up huge bills he couldn't pay networking with moustachioed guys. They always had screen names like Jimbo and Pee Wee. ReCon Surgery Inc will be reclaiming pieces of Petey's face by the end of the year; he's so behind in repayments.

After I have eaten, I sink into my bed in the darkness and wait for it to be time to go to work again.

In the morning, I am woken by Petey's hair dryer, an hour before my alarm goes off. He doesn't have to be up for anything. Clients almost always come around in the evenings. He just likes to start his beauty regime early.

Today is special. When I get to work, Lance is unpacking the latest arrival. Beneath the bubble wrap is the newest Continuum XY cartridge, fresh in from the States.

"This is gonna be sweet," Lance informs me, with a smirk, "You want first trial?"

I pick through the packing material and find the game manual.

"Beat 'em up?" I am unimpressed. I can just about stand a zombie splattering gore fest, but judging by the instruction booklet, this is straightforward martial arts. For knuckleheads. "I'll pass," I tell Lance, handing the manual over, "I'm gonna log in."

"All work and no play make Max a dull... person," he teases. I stick my fingers up at him and turn to stow my bag under the counter. "You gotta try this Max," Lance persists, "It's got some pukka new tech. Just give it a go, you'll love it."

Before I know it, I'm strapped into the Continuum, waiting with gritted teeth for the brief stabbing headache as the game is forced into my brain. It doesn't come. The game loads so smoothly, it's hard to tell I'm in it. I only realise I am when I look down and see that the trodes are gone from my arms. They are still there, in the real world, but inside this construction, there's no need for them.

The menu appears in front of me, a solid silver vending machine in the centre of the wooden laminate floor. I study the options: Quickstart, Multi-play, Customise Opponent. I press Customise, and the room changes seamlessly. A blank droid sits on a chair in place of the vending machine. Facial features, hairstyles, clothing and colour swatches line the walls. As I press each feature, it appears on the droid.

I work away, enjoying the depth and detail of the customisation. Finally, my opponent is ready. From his coiffured yellow hair to his distressed denim baseball boots, he's perfect. He's Petey.

I spend hours working Petey's beautiful face into a pulp with my fists, watching the super-realistic blood fly. A voice bank of over a thousand vocal imprints means even the characters' agonised groans sound just like Petey's would. I savour feeling his bones crunch beneath my fists, really feeling it. And when Petey is too battered and broken to go on, the game has him on autosave, and so he respawns and I can fight him again. Even better than the real thing.

The Real Thing

In the end, Lance has to come in and get me. I'm half an hour late for my shift.

Over the next few weeks, I find more amazing details in the game. The fighting area can be customised too. I give it a scuffed grey linoleum floor, sour-milk coloured storage units and appliances and a dish filled sink, just like our kitchen. I change the settings on my opponent. Some days he fights back - karate, kickboxing, judo. Other days, he stands meek as a lamb and lets the blows rain down on his sculpted face.

So that's how I came to be beating on Petey. It keeps me sane. I can smilingly do all his dishes, scrub the tea-stains from his mugs, scrape the splattered gunk from the microwave, because I've spent the past few hours watching the life ebb from those turquoise eyes again and again.

Then, one night, I get home and there's no stranger in the bathroom. I go to turn on the light, and there's no light. A pile of unpaid bills lie on the table. Petey again. He hoards all our letters, only permitting me to see them when he's good and ready. I flip through the pile, finding the utility bills and a letter addressed to me. It has Premier A stamped on the envelope. I hope it's informing me of another Employee of the Month award and gaming voucher and decide to save it, to open it later in the privacy of my room. Not that Petey seems to be around. Hopefully he's moved out without telling me, like the last guy.

I gather the dirty plates from the table. Some have been lurking under Petey's bed so long they're furred with mould. Whistling a tune, I fill the sink with hot water. The tune is one I programmed into the game. It's full of crashing guitars and violent drum beats; an ideal accompaniment to pounding a pretty face against a kitchen countertop.

The intense heat of the water makes me wince as it rushes into the cuts and scrapes on my knuckles. Maybe I've been playing the game a little *too* much. Lance warned me to lay off last week. I overrun a couple of lunch breaks by half an hour or so and the guy goes ballistic. Seems to forget all the unpaid hours I put in over the last few months.

When the dishes are done, I wipe my heat-reddened hands on the dishcloth, turn towards my room, and trip, falling full length over a pile of clothes Petey has left on the floor in front of the washer. I am about to scoop them up and sling them into Petey's room, cursing his laziness when I realise what I am really looking at.

Glassy turquoise eyes and blood soaked yellow hair.

My stomach constricts and I gag, vomit burning my throat but refusing to leave my body. On my knees, I rip open the envelope from

Premier A and scan the page, needing something, something to make this better.

Dismissal. Unprofessional behaviour. Excessive personal use of company property.

I slump to the floor, and lie foetal, inches away from Petey. He smells of blood and fear. His eight thousand euro face is fractured as a Picasso painting. And he won't respawn. He won't be standing over a bathroom stranger tomorrow night, or the next, or the next. I don't understand it. He always, always gets up.

EGGS

Mahendra Solanki

I make the dish you made.
Eggs, spiced with
nuggets of red chilli,
catching my breath.

Each plate is stained
like my fingers with
turmeric, forever marked.

CRACKING

Jennie Wallace

Third floor, second right, straight down the corridor, past the water cooler: Room 309B. He felt he could find his way blindfold. Two fifty five. Bobby slowed his step. There was no point in arriving early, no one liked to be unduly surprised.

Pausing before he opened the door, he forced a smile. The same morose expression greeted him, and once more Bobby bit back a sigh of despair.

"Is she here?" came the muttered voice, startling him.

The man sitting in the chair rarely talked and Bobby, with all his skills and training, had been unable to find an opening into the mind that lay behind the closed, passive exterior. He squared his shoulders and smiled at the sullen, unresponsive face before him.

"Of course she's here, Chris. You don't think Minna would miss today do you?" Spoken in a confident, reassuring voice.

Hearing the door creak, Bobby's head whipped round so fast he heard his neck crack. His face crumpled into relief when Minna walked in. He noticed that she looked better than she had in weeks; the dark circles around her eyes were beginning to clear and her lovely olive skin had a real glow. Bobby bit back the compliment he would like to have given. Her visits to Christopher inevitably caused stress, but she was the only one he would tolerate. At times Bobby believed Christopher almost liked him too; at times.

Immediately a smile blossomed on Christopher's face. Bobby was amazed at the difference; for once he actually looked his age, a sixteen year old, not the querulous, miserable old-man look he'd been cultivating since he arrived. Smiling suited him.

"Are you OK?" she asked, "I've brought you a present." Christopher seemed to genuinely consider the question before he answered.

"You're here. I'm fine," he grinned. He looked like an excited little boy, Bobby mused. He felt his heart constrict a little with emotion, and further with concern that this involvement was perhaps unprofessional. Minna had relaxed visibly at the statement.

She smiled at her brother as she clasped his hand. Minna was the only one allowed to touch him.

"I hate this fucking hell hole," he murmured to her, glancing around the room. Bobby privately agreed; the cheerful, brightly coloured room seemed to jar the senses. Minna's eyes took in for the hundredth time the family photographs, a few dusty books and his parents' favourite classic CDs, all in all a piss-poor selection of objects. Minna's eyebrows knitted together in confusion at a new picture on the wall.

"When d'you get *that*?" she asked, pointing to the figure. Christopher shrugged. "Something mum and dad gave me. He looks like a hippie, I hate him. I tried to get rid of the picture but they wouldn't let me, they wouldn't tell me why." He turned away.

Bobby's mouth would have dropped in disbelief, but he prided himself on his self-control, so his jaw didn't move. Not *once* since arriving had Chris spoken so much.

"Why do you hate him?" she whispered, leaning closer as she stroked his head. The thick, dark hair had been cut into a more structured style. She smoothed it back away from his forehead, something she had done since they were little; it always relaxed him.

"He looks like a ghost ready to suck my soul. His arms are always open but he won't welcome me; he always smiles, he loves us all, but they say he hates the way I love. His eyes follow me around the room but he never really *sees* me. He pretends to be good but he frightens me. He always wears white, I hate white," he murmured, suddenly beginning to feel drowsy.

"Here's your present," she grinned, fishing in her pocket before she dragged out a photograph. "I meant to show you yesterday but you were asleep when I came."

"I wish you'd woken me, I like seeing you. I miss you."

"You need your sleep," she chastised gently. At times like this he forgot Minna's age. She'd had to grow up too quickly and he felt somehow guilty for that.

Taking in the photo he smiled at the image of the blond boy, proudly clutching a teddy, a toothy smile for the camera. Had he ever looked like that as a kid? He doubted it somehow. He didn't think he'd ever smiled, not like that. Finn was lucky to have Minna. She loved her little boy unconditionally; they had each other, whereas he had nobody. Well, he had Minna, that was true and perhaps Bobby, but they were busy. They had their own lives while he was stuck here, day after day. He'd lost everything, even Evan had been taken away. His parents said Evan was the one who made him sick. He didn't see how though. Evan had been his best friend, he'd never hurt Christopher, he loved him. Christopher knew that.

He'd been promised he'd get better soon but he was beginning to wonder if they were lying. Maybe he was dying and they didn't want to tell him. That would make sense.

"Mum and Dad send their love and they'll call you later on tonight; they'll use the tele-link. Finn wants to see you. He really misses you, they all do."

He choked down the tears threatening to spill. *Boys don't cry,* he reminded himself. W*e're strong. I'm strong.* Suddenly a man appeared in the doorway and Minna sighed.

"Sorry, I have to go now Chris. They won't let me stay for very long anymore, I don't know why."

Placing a kiss on his temple she wrapped her arms around him, before she whispered in his ear, "Happy birthday little brother," and the man escorted her out.

Minna was gone. She was free to come and go as she pleased, not stuck here with doctors fussing around her; she got to see Finn grow up, saw a world he was locked away from. He turned to the calendar hanging on his wall. This birthday was circled in red: 25th December 2021. Tomorrow. Mum and Dad said it was a special day, not only for him but he shared it with another very special man. They'd been so happy with their special boy born on a special day to such special parents. Minna only just missed the miracle, being a few minutes older. It was Christopher who was special by a minute.

Not only that, but this birthday was a significant one. He was sixteen; legal. He didn't need his parents' 'protection', he was a free man, and he could get out of this sterile hellhole as soon as possible; he just needed to sign the papers and he would be free. Free. The thought alone was enough to make him delirious with happiness. *Happy fucking birthday to me.*

He was so wrapped up in his thoughts he didn't see Bobby silently slip out of the door, a sad smile playing around his lips. Christopher's body seemed to fold back in on itself; its brief time of animation was over. Until Minna visited again he was alone with his thoughts. They were his, no-one could take them away, and Evan was part of those thoughts. Glancing up, his eye caught the small TV screen nestling in a corner; the eyes and ears of the room. Nothing could be hidden here, as with every other room in this building, except for thoughts.

A woman in a white coat, walking towards Christopher's room, stopped Bobby.

"Any change in the patient Dr Hamid?" she asked, concern evident in her voice. The nurse was obviously new.

"Just Bobby," he explained. At the woman's confused expression, he elaborated: "I'm known as Bobby here, it makes the patients feel safer. No coats, no uniforms, it's one of our rules. It makes it easier for them to trust us, makes us easier to relate to. If you'll excuse me I need to check on Minna."

He was still concerned as to how her visit to Christopher had affected her emotionally. Walking down the corridor, he nodded at the guard.

"How was she?" he queried.

"She didn't give us any problems this time, sir. They're both still having the nightmares but the sedatives you gave them are working. I think she's a lot more highly strung than she was showing us to begin with."

"Good. I'm assuming you don't need me around tonight?" asked Bobby; the guard nodded crisply, and Dr Hamid wearily made his way down the corridor.

Bobby had come to the conclusion long ago that he liked Christopher. Unlike so many here, Chris had spark and fire that he seldom saw in his line of work. True, it was a quiet, slow-burning fire. He was fighting the system in his own way. It grieved Bobby to see a life so full of potential being tethered in such a fashion, and so unnecessarily, so perversely. Not that he would share his views with the rest of the medical community, or the community at large. They would undoubtedly revoke his medical licence for such a slanderous comment.

The law stated that Christopher Oxford was clinically insane, and whether Bobby privately disagreed was irrelevant. He was hired to treat his patient, to give him the required medicines and tick the relevant boxes. That was all. And besides, the Brotherhood had subsidised his medical training and supported his application for this job ... well, the Brotherhood had everyone's interests at heart. The publicity material in the recruitment pack came flooding back to him.

People did not always know what was good for them; they were fallible, selfish; they made foolish decisions. The Brotherhood simply provided that much needed morality and guidance so many young people lacked. People were grateful for it, grateful that the Atlantic Alliance of 2008 had paved the way for the Brotherhood. Of course, not everyone had always welcomed their policies, especially the recent, and some would have argued more radical ideas, but with the benefit of hindsight it was acknowledged that such drastic steps had been needed, and society was all the better for it.

Walking to his office, Bobby was greeted by Maggie, his secretary. She smiled wanly at him.

"Bobby, Mr and Mrs Oxford are here," she said, a small sigh escaping her lips. Bobby found himself wondering what Maggie was doing here; at only twenty-four, surely she was too young to have such a world-weary expression? But then, wasn't he too young at the grand age of thirty-two to be such a cynic. Of course, children grew up more quickly now. A ten year old was no longer a child; adolescence marked not the beginning of a wilderness but a loss of innocence, an immersion into the hard, real world. Society no longer indulged adolescent mistakes, blaming hormones or rap music. People paid the price for their mistakes, just like Christopher and Minna.

Mr and Mrs Oxford. Christopher's parents. This was becoming a ritual of sorts. Every month they would demand, or rather *enquire* of their son's wellbeing, whether any progress had been made. Each month it was the same:

"As for change Mr and Mrs Oxford, I'm afraid it's just not happening. His condition is stable, and his body is slowly responding to the drug therapy but his mind remains unaffected. I can give him the most powerful drugs the government allows but it will not alter Christopher's mind. Science cannot interfere with the brain in such a way, not without causing irrevocable damage in the process. Christopher must cure himself."

Despite his professional demeanour, Bobby felt a perverse satisfaction at speaking those words. Mr and Mrs Oxford were loving parents. Everyone could see how loving they were. People expressed no end of pity for them, that their two children should end up in this state. Everyone openly congratulated them on taking such a brave but necessary step. They were not Bobby's concern. He only had to deal with them once a month to give a report that never altered, to see Mrs Oxford's eyes flood with tears, Mr Oxford's jaw tick; it was such a well rehearsed routine Bobby felt they could do it blindfolded.

He noticed they rarely enquired after Minna, perhaps their concern was not as great, or perhaps Minna's sins far outweighed Christopher's. After all, Christopher could renounce his. All he had to do was renounce Evan and his life would be his own again. But how did one reject love? Bobby had never had an answer for that.

Minna and Christopher both shared the sin of love. Minna's love was for the wrong man, and her love for her son Finn had brought her here. There was no brushing away of this sin. Finn was flesh and blood, a tangible symbol of Minna's 'fall from grace'. The child was as much of a sign as the lack of a gold band around her finger. That band would have secured society's blessings. Now due to its absence she was branded mad and locked away. She could not renounce her love for Finn.

Mr and Mrs Oxford got up, pain shining in their eyes. Bobby refused to feel pity for them and, carefully masking his emotions, he showed them out. Before they exited Mrs Oxford turned to Bobby and handed him a photo, lips trembling.

"Please give this to Minna. It was Finn's birthday yesterday. Two candles already. He's not her little baby anymore,"

Bobby nodded slightly as he took in the photo. He swallowed the bile threatening to rise up. Time to get some sleep.

"I'll see she gets it," he promised.

So now both twins had a photograph. Christopher's was not the picture of the deity his parents insisted hung on his wall, but the deity carefully hidden under his bed. A worn image of two boys, both perhaps fourteen years of age. Love and happiness in their faces. A girl sat by them, a blinding grin on her face. They didn't have a care in the world, for none knew their world would be destroyed in a matter of months. Christopher thought no one knew about the photo, he went to great pains to hide it, but Bobby knew and so did Minna. They knew everything about each other.

It was for love Minna and Christopher kept each other's secrets and protected each other from their harsh realities. It was for love that their parents put them both here, and for love that the Brotherhood insisted they stay. It was love that made Evan and Christopher risk everything and pay a heavy price, Evan with a casket and Christopher with his freedom.

Bobby thought love was overrated.

REVOLVING DOORS: A PRISON DIARY

Phil Bond

This is the diary of Jamie Wilson from Moss Side, Manchester, written so that one day everyone will read it and think what a fuckin deep and complicated soul I am.

14th December
The problem with me is that even though I've been off the skag for a couple of years, I've never quite been able to shake off the mentality that I got from them days of nickin' everything that isn't nailed down. I just can't help meself, that's how I ended up in here. Vicky said to us when I got sent down, "you've got a choice: pack in the nicking or pack in us". Of course there's only gonna be one choice outta that - gotta get your priorities right, don't ya? So I told her to go fuck herself! Nah, only messing. She's top, Vicky is, had the best year of me life with her, I don't wanna mess things up. I told her I was gonna go straight, make sure I don't end up back in here, and I meant what I said. At the time I did, anyways.

In association I got chatting with Sparksy, this rat-faced kid from the next block. Massive United fan, so a wanker by definition. Told him that I was getting released from this shit-hole on the 21st. Suddenly he gets all interested, tells us he's out on the 22nd, and asks if I'd be interested in a bit of business. The amount of schemes and plans that fly about in here, it's like a think tank for crime. I tell him that I'm Mr Legit now, me bird's gonna rip me balls off if I get in any more shit. He goes to us, "let me tell you a joke, son: what do you say to a bird with two black eyes? You don't need to say nowt, you've already told her twice!" The shit that comes outta this kid's mouth, what a knob-jockey! I told him, "You should meet me bird. If I punched her she would kick two shades outta me!" He looked at me like I was talking rubbish, but anyone who knows Vicky would know exactly what I'm on about.

I probably shoulda just walked off then, but old habits die hard, and I was curious about what he was lining up. He tells us he needs someone to help him doin' over rich cunts' houses on Christmas Eve in the posh parts of Manchester, while they're all away at Midnight Mass! I laughed at this cos I thought he was taking the piss, but he reckons that it'll be a proper easy way to make a shit-load of cash. He says to us, "how are you expecting to buy anyone a Christmas present outta the £12.50 they give ya when you leave this place? You talk about your bird dumping ya, but how's she gonna react when all you can afford to give her is a tin of beans from Netto?" This is something that I've already thought about. There's a lot of pressure on ya being released just before Chrimbo, the time of year when you need money the most. So I start opening me ears a bit more to what he's saying. He goes on, "the best thing bout this job, we can shift all the T.V.'s and that from the houses for cash, and also half inch all the people's presents already wrapped. You'll bird'll ride you like her life depends on it when you hand her some of that fancy shit. The rest of it we'll shift on with the other stuff, which'll mean we should get a few ton coming back at us. You could take your bird out to a right swanky restaurant, celebrate New Year's in some proper style. Or you could be a sad bastard and sit at home on your own while everyone else is out partying, cos you don't have a pot to piss in!"

Old habits, they die harder than Bruce fuckin' Willis.

16th December

No exercise today cos the weather was shit. Something not right about going a whole forty-eight hours without fresh air: just a dank, sweating, piss-soaked stench.

Sharing a cell with Billy is mint in some ways. He's bout thirty-five or thirty-six, so he's got over a decade's more experience than me, and he's good to talk to bout stuff. I like listening to him and the other older lads telling stories bout how everything used to be round Manchester. Told him bout this job I'm probably gonna do on Christmas Eve, he goes, "you're a fuckin' bell-end for even talking to that scumbag Sparksy! Let me tell ya Jamie, Christmas in Strangeways ain't exactly all holiday cheer!"

The bad thing about bunking with Bill is that he's a smackhead. Like 90% of the inmates here. That's why so many inmates re-offend after being released, the 'revolving doors system' as Billy calls it. People leave prison, start stealing even more, taking bigger risks, cos now on top of everything else they've got a raging smack habit to support. I've not even really wanted the stuff since I got with Vicky, but bein' in here brings back all that animal fuckin' craving for it. Every single day, someone'll come in here and offer me some. Couple of times it's been really difficult to say no. Last night, after lights out, I was trying to get to sleep, but Bill was chasing the dragon (as he does every night). When I tasted that old familiar sweet, sugary smell in me lungs I was more tempted than a paedophile in a nursery. But I can't go back to them days, man, they were the lowest. Looking at the picture of Vicky on me cupboard, the one where her tits look well nice, makes me strong enough to resist the temptation.

I can't wait to get outta here! On the phone today, hearing her Jessica Rabbit voice (if you can imagine Jessica Rabbit with a Manc accent) telling me she loved me made me miss her so much its unbearable. I wanna get back playing with the band again 'n' all, write some new songs with Tony. I've got plenty of killer lyrics to use from things I've seen in here. Eyeball to eyeball, that's how me and him write, just like Lennon and McCartney in their early days. He's a mint frontman, Tony is, and I reckon I've got me own style on guitar which makes us a real force to be reckoned with. I'm John Squire to his Ian Brown, Keith Richards to his Mick Jagger. I dunno why he hasn't been to see us in here. I suppose it must be pretty weird to see your best mate behind bars, caged up like some fuckin' animal. I'm not gonna end up back in here again, though, that's for sure. I'm off on the straight and narrow from now on. Right after I do this job with Sparksy, get a bit of money to send us on me way. Then no more.

17th December

Me mum came to visit us today. Stupidly mentioned that I've turned Muslim in here. It's the only way to get nice grub, if you're a Muslim you get proper nice chicken and lentils and that. It's definitely a better option than them dodgy meat pies, you never know what's in them! Anyway, me mum got pretty arsey 'bout this, said that I was betraying me Catholic roots. I was like - "Alright mum, it's hardly like we're in the front row at St Michaels every week, is it?" - which, being the melodramatic she is, made her get out her handkerchief and wipe away an invisible tear. Despite the argument it was good to see her. I'd take a bit of me mum's home cooking over any of the shit they serve in here, Muslim or not, any day of the week.

After me mum went I headed over to Sparksy's cell to finalise the plans. He reckons most people won't leave their alarms on - "After all," he said, "who would expect to get robbed on Christmas Eve?" This got us thinking for the first time about how harsh it is robbing people the night before Christmas. Imagine the disappointment for the kids when their presents have disappeared. It reminds me of that Christmas when I was about ten, and we went over to me dad's house for a couple of hours after we had the turkey and everything. He got us all a Teenage Mutant Ninja Turtle toy each, and I got Raphael, me favourite ('cos he was a proper lad, but deep at the same time). Then me mum smashed it to pieces on Boxing Day as a punishment after I battered our Kev. I was well mardy 'bout that, and that's how I'm probably gonna make some kids feel next week. But fuck it, I can't afford to be thinking like that. At the end of the day, they've got money and I haven't, they'll be able to replace those presents. I hope so anyway.

18th December
Me one blessing in here is that I've actually got a telly in me cell, so me and Bill watch the soaps and that, which I think is the one thing keeping me sane. It almost makes up for how cold it is.

Tried ringing Vicky today, she wasn't there so I rang Tony instead. He was a bit quiet at first, I think he was feeling bad about not coming to visit or write me or nowt. I asked him, sort of jokingly, whether the band had been up to much while I've been inside. He told me that they'd done a couple of sessions with his mate Blackie playing guitar, which pissed me off, but I never said nowt. I told him we're gonna have a big night out Monday for me release, which he said he was up for. He sounded a bit off with me, like he was distracted or something - maybe he's got family problems again. He's one of the best, Tone is. After I get the money for this job I'll buy him a few pints and we'll rip it up in town, just like the old days.

19th December
Couldn't really sleep last night, just thinking bout everything. It didn't help that Billy was snoring louder that me Auntie Coleen after a few whiskies. I tried waking him, partly to stop the snoring and also cos I wanted to talk with him, but it was like trying to wake a shot down elephant. I might've thought he had OD'd if it wasn't for the hideous sound, like a blocked up drain, coming from the back of his throat.

On heavy rotation in my thoughts were Vicky, this place, me mum, this job with Sparksy, and all that, so me mind was racing too much to go to sleep. I kept thinking 'bout how I ended up in here. It wasn't even as if it were a big job or nowt, I was just nicking Vicky some perfume that she wanted. It would've been alright, but when I saw that security guard grab her, I just lost it, smacked him straight in the Adams apple. I might not've even got a sentence if I hadn't've done that. There's just something 'bout that girl, I'd fight anyone for her 'cos I love her so much. But what if we get caught on this job? She'll go ballistic, probably finish with us. The last thing I want is to be spending Christmas back in here. But Sparksy reckons there isn't much risk of being caught, as there's gonna be less rozzers about on duty than usual, with it being Christmas Eve and all. I need the money, though. I NEED the fuckin' money!

20th December
Gonna leave Strangeways forever in ten hours' time, unless the bastard wardens have messed up the paperwork for me release. Feel like I should be really taking in these final hours, make me freedom all the sweeter. To be honest, though, I can't be released soon enough, I hate it in here so much. I can't wait to shag Vicky, when I think about all the things I'm gonna do to her it gets me harder than a frozen sausage.

I went over this morning and told Sparksy I was out, that I can't afford to take the risk. He tried to talk me back in, calling me all the pussies under the sun. Me mind's been made up and nowt can change it. I'll be skint when I come outta here, but that's alright. Tony and people will sort me out with a bit of cash, a few pints. I just can't gamble me relationship with Vicky over this, she deserves better than a jailbird boyfriend. And I don't think that I could take another stint in here, it's not the holiday camp that everyone says it is. Fuckin' hell, Butlins must've really gone downhill since I were a kid. I'd say on a scale of camps it's closer to a concentration camp. Time to say a few goodbyes, I won't be meeting up with anyone from here on the outside. They're good, honest lads, but I just don't wanna be reminded.

Billy told me when you leave this place, the wardens tell ya that they'll keep your cell warm for you. That ain't gonna happen to me, I can guarantee that! Next time I write an entry in here, if I ever need to again, I will be a free man with the bird of me dreams on me arm.

23rd December
Rick's lying to me I know he is it can't be true I've gotta calm the fuck down it can't be true. Why is he saying bullshit like that? Just calm down Jamie go and talk to her she'll tell you it's not true calm down. No. Go and speak to him get him to tell you it's not true…

24th December
Is there anybody stupider in the whole entire world than me? Back after two days. How I got on my high horse saying no to the job with Sparksy, and tomorrow he'll be living it up with shit loads of cash while I'll be caged up in here. On my own. Don't even have a fuckin' telly this time.

How can she live with herself? And Tony, me supposed best mate, stabbing me in the back, shagging me bird the whole time I was inside. I get a panic attack when I think of them together. I hate her, and I hate him. But most of all I hate meself, I'm the one that hammered the nail in me own coffin. I should've just kept it together, walked away and planned how to get that cunt back in the rational light of day. I just fuckin lost it though, couldn't stop hitting him even when the rozzers turned up. There's no chance I'll get bail, especially cos I was tagged - I'm gonna be back in this hell for a while.

I've gotta numb the pain, in the only way I know how.

25th December
I feel groggy as fuck, I forgot how much the gear knocks you out. I was wasted last night, me tolerance has gone to shit, but it has been a long time since I done it. It made me puke everywhere, but after that I felt miles better. Just didn't care as much. I feel awful again now though, gotta find some more from somewhere. I've just seen what I wrote on the wall last night – I've got a new heroine. Shows what a mess I was.

I keep thinking, cos there's nowt else to do in here but think, bout what Billy was on about with the revolving doors system. I thought it was only drugs that got people caught up in those revolving doors, but I was wrong. She's the one that's imprisoned me, not any rozzers.

Me mum's coming to visit us later, but I can't face her. I've let her down too much. Fuck this is horrible. If there is a God out there I wish to fuck that he would help me. I'm gonna go and score.

Later entry: Just seen Sparksy being hauled in here. At least that's some fuckin' consolation.

IT'S SATURDAY NIGHT

Maxine Linnell

Auntie Betty puts some of her lipstick on my mouth. I've never had lipstick before. I feel awkward, with my lips pushed out. The lipstick smells of perfume, and it feels like dripping. I want to lick it off right away, eat it.

On Friday nights I sleep with prickly hair rollers. At least I try to sleep. It's Saturday today, so I'm really tired, I've got curls shaped like rollers and my scalp's raw. I'm wearing an outfit I've made myself, from a Simplicity pattern. Navy top and skirt, with bright green borders. Flat shoes, saggy stockings that make my legs feel funny, NHS glasses. I don't much like being a girl, never have. But I'm doing my best.

Auntie Betty makes me wear a headscarf too, pulled forward over my face. It lies on the curls, like a shroud.

I have to look older, because the film we're going to is an X, adults only. I'm not happy about it. I can't tell my mum. She wouldn't let me stay with Auntie Betty if she knew. But Auntie Betty says she really wants me to see this film. It's important, she says.

Uncle Dick gives Auntie Betty a look, like he's not sure about it. He's not coming.

"Just us girls," says Auntie Betty, but she doesn't look much like a girl. She won't listen to me worrying about being caught out by the box office lady. I never look seventeen; I was only twelve last month.

Auntie Betty clutches my hand under her elbow as we leave the house. I dread being found out all the way to the pictures. I stand in the queue, cheeks red-hot, eyes glued to my shoes. I can't tell if the lady looks at me to see if I'm old enough. I don't look up, just follow Auntie's shoes up the carpet, past the usherette, into the dark cinema that smells of old cigarettes and popcorn.

We have to walk down past the back rows. They're already full, the couples are always in the queue first, then the men run off to get the double seats. Tonight, because we were late with the lipstick and everything, the couples are sitting there, lined up, men's arms hung round the girls' shoulders, like they're waiting for the lights to go out. I hope they don't miss the film. I wouldn't like to go to the pictures and miss the film. Once in a quiet bit I heard a girl from the back say "Stop it, Jeff," really loud. People giggled. Auntie Betty snorted. I wanted to look round but I didn't.

It's Saturday Night

I love the pictures. We go every Saturday, except if it's an X, which makes this week different. I love the news, the adverts, the B movie, even standing up for the queen at the end. We settle in. There's chocolate. With Auntie Betty there's always chocolate. I have a Bounty and I begin to feel better.

The main film is called Saturday Night and Sunday Morning. It's black and white. It's a film about a town like mine, my dark redbrick home. It's about now, not the past, not some fairytale; people older than me, exciting people.

Arthur, the hero, is a James Dean Elvis Presley man. He's a man man, not a boy man. I love his anger, the chip on his broad shoulders, his longing for something better.

"I'd like to see anybody grind me down. I'm out for a good time."

I want a good time too, so much. I don't know what it is, but I know I want it. I want to be Arthur. I want to be bad and not care. When somebody shouts at me I want to laugh at them. I'm leaning forward and the woman behind pokes me on the shoulder and hisses at me: "Sit back, I can't see".

I slump down in my seat. I don't care. Auntie Betty nudges my elbow hard and I sit up again, but I take my time.

I've never seen anyone drunk before. My dad has a bottle of brown ale on Saturdays. He believes in giving us a taste to try. I hate mine. When Arthur gets drunk, it looks great. Even when he falls down the stairs, he smiles before he falls asleep on the floor. I love him, I do.

I've watched kissing on films, at a distance, after a proper proposal. I asked my mum what French kissing was when I found it in a library book. She looked at me for a bit, then said, "It's beautiful when you're married."

Beautiful when you're married. That makes no sense at all. How could something so stupid and disgusting turn beautiful because you got married?

I don't know much else about what happens when you get married, so it's a shock to see Arthur with Brenda, who turns out to be married to Jack. Jack is Arthur's friend at work. Arthur and Brenda are in bed together doing something which looks like French kissing. It kind of melts my stomach when I see them.

Arthur keeps saying how he won't get married till he's good and ready. I know how he feels. Looking at my mum and dad I can't see any reason to get married. Unless you want to find out what being bored and lonely feels like, forever.

Then Brenda gets pregnant. I know about love and marriage and getting pregnant. They should come in that order. Of course, Brenda isn't happy, with a husband and a son already. She yells about being sick and fat, kids screaming and getting no sleep. I don't think Arthur likes her so much now. She tries to get rid of it, she drinks gin and sits in a hot bath for three hours. I wonder how the water stays hot that long. Then she decides to have the baby and take what comes.

She's obviously not for Arthur, she's Jack's wife. They'll end it now. He'll be all right, and he and Doreen can have a good time and get married and everything. I start my second bar of chocolate, a Crunchie this time. I have to suck it so it doesn't make a noise. My tongue goes all crinkly when I stick it in the honeycomb part.

Then things get worse. There's the fair. Arthur's with Doreen. She's young and pretty. Her hair's all wavy and wears a tight belt and a flared out skirt. I bet she doesn't need prickly hair rollers. If I can't be Arthur I want to be Doreen. She's flying round the waltzers and the dodgems with Arthur, like I went round them in Blackpool last year with my friend.

Then Brenda sees Arthur at the fair. There's the moment he meets up with her, the moment they go on the ride, his arm around her, Jack's soldier brothers watching, biding their time, waiting. The moment they catch him. The moment they beat him up. I've never seen fighting like fighting, the clumsiness of it, the dirt of it. I feel sick. It hurts. Poor Arthur's in bed for a week.

I want to go home now, but one look at my aunt says no. We have to sit it out. Not long now till the queen. I have a look at my shoes: it always helps when you want to cry.

When Arthur gives in, when he promises Doreen a ring, he's not happy, you can see that. I bet he'll only buy her a cheap one. And she turns all sensible and critical, before the ring is on her finger. She wants a new house, with a bathroom. It's all over.

I'm crying when it ends. I stumble to my feet for the queen and rub my eyes under my glasses. I've eaten the lipstick off and dropped tears all down my flat front.

My arm is jammed under Auntie Betty's as we walk home. I nearly have to run to keep up. I have nothing to say. I'm not sure I'll ever say anything again. As my aunt reaches up to unlock the door, she turns and says briskly, "So now you know. You remember, right? Let that film be a lesson to you."

I feel like I've lost something. I don't know what it is, but it's gone. But there's something else. I feel like I've joined a special new club, one I didn't know about before.

I look up into Auntie Betty's eyes for the first time. She smiles at me and winks.

"No need to tell your uncle. He wouldn't understand."

I wipe my nose on my coat sleeve and follow Auntie Betty inside.

A PIGEON IN THE ATTIC

Rosemary Brierley

From the top of the house, I watch the snowflakes. By morning the garden will be shrouded in white. White is my colour. I wear it now; I wore it then, in the house that became my life. The house I will never leave.

At fourteen, I stood in the street and gazed up at the polished brass between the stained glass panels of the double front doors. I remember how the gate in the wrought-iron railings resisted my first timid attempt to push it open. Then, when I summoned up courage and used all the force I could muster, it groaned and swung wide, leaving me clutching the metal spikes, teetering above a narrow basement courtyard. There was no handrail as I descended below pavement level. On one side, the treads were hardly sufficient for a footprint, on the other they dwindled to nothing as the stone staircase curved round, to the small door beneath the wide marble steps.

I remember how my legs quivered as I stood there and knocked. When the door opened I was barely able to speak, just pointed to the newspaper clutched in my hand and whispered, "My name is Edith."

The housekeeper provided the white pinafores, almost to my ankles, and the white mop cap: the clothes reserved for when I was visible, scurrying to answer the bell or waiting at table. When no one saw me, as I polished the parquet floor, black-leaded the range, or battled with posser and peggy-tub, I wore a more serviceable dark grey. Now, although I wear white all the time, I am always invisible.

I slept on a lumpy mattress, on an old iron bedstead in one of the small distempered rooms at the front under the gables. In winter, at five o'clock, when I crawled from beneath the blankets to lay the fires, there was ice on the inside of the tiny window and my breath froze in a cloud. Now I don't feel the cold. I reside among the stored furniture, the tin trunks and discarded toys, in the attic at the back of the house.

The housekeeper's gone. There are no staff. Now "Magic Maids" arrive, in their pink van, once a fortnight. They unload the mechanical floor polisher, whip round with the Hoover and switch the automatic oven to self-clean.

The master, his wife and four daughters are long gone. The house has passed down to his grandson. Geoffrey Bradley is a solicitor in the city; his wife, Marion, does voluntary work. Their two elder daughters, now in their thirties, have husbands and children. Only Zoe, born to the couple much later in life, still lives at home.

"It's snowing. If the buses aren't running, you'll have to walk to work," Marion calls to her daughter, Zoe.

Zoe says, "OK", but has no intention of emerging from beneath the duvet.

Ten minutes later, wearing only a large shapeless tee shirt, her bare feet making no sound on the fitted carpet, she crosses the landing to the bathroom. No point in irritating her mother, not after last night!

They both decide not to resurrect the argument, not to mention Colin. Marion bites her lip and resolves not to say yet again, "He's old enough to be your father." Zoe is not wearing the engagement ring.

Instead they talk of trivialities.

"Did you hear a noise in the night?" asks Zoe. "I think it came from the loft... a kind of fluttering."

"Might be a pigeon," replies her mother. They get in under the eaves then can't get out. I'll go up later on."

Marion, her hair tied up in a scarf, comes into the attic. She shines her torch around the small compartment just inside the entrance. In its beam, she identifies the girls' cuddly toys, still loved but no longer needed, the ring binders bulging with the once studied Xeroxed handouts, Aunt Mary's dinner service, which might be worth something one day. But there are no tell tale feathers or droppings.

The family only ever comes in here to deposit the discarded, or retrieve the remembered. They have never ventured through the hole in the brickwork to reach the darker, dustier rear of the attic. To get there, the living have to crawl on all fours. Once through, Marion straightens up and brushes the cobwebs from her face. The faint flutter she thinks she hears – she's not sure – is coming from the far end, where the joists meet the rafters. But the floor is not boarded; between the exposed joists is just lath and plaster. Marion knows that one false step will result in an expensive repair to the bedroom ceiling below.

The thought of a trapped being spurs her on: balancing on two feet at first, then crouching, then crawling. Did the noise come from here? She directs the torch into the far corner. Nothing but an old trunk. The locks rusted with age, she doesn't expect them to yield to the pressure of her thumbs. But they do. She gazes down on the neatly folded clothes and picks up a leather-bound volume, with gilt corners, then prises the clasp open. In spidery writing on the flyleaf is the name *Mary James.*

It is cold in the attic and growing colder. She is pleased she had the forethought to wear her gardening jacket and huddles inside it. As she opens the diary a slight draught flutters the pages, causing her to make a mental note to get the builders to check the roof. The recent storms were severe enough to dislodge goodness knows how many tiles on a house of this age. She shines her torch on the yellowing paper.

June 12th 1947.
We were married today. John said I looked beautiful in the cream silk suit that Edith and I made, in secret, in her tiny room in the attic. Edith has been a staunch ally over the last few months. She was the only one who knew when we left. I didn't even write to my sisters. They still think of me as the baby of the family, even though I'm nearly twenty-three. They would disapprove, just like Mother and Father.

Edith wished us all the best. Said what did it matter if John is forty-five. Anyway nowadays, eligible bachelors are quickly snapped up. I feel so sorry for Edith; Archie never came back from Dunkirk. She says she will never marry.

As Marion leafs through the diary, no dust rises from the pages.

Sept 8th 1955.
We went to see them today. Edith wrote to say Father's not been well. It was hard to explain to Amy why she's never seen her grandparents before. She was shy and, for most of the time, followed Edith around with a duster. When we left, Father shook John's hand. They promised to visit, when the new baby is born.

The front door slams. Marion starts, hits her head on the rafters and drops the diary. Feeling around in the darkness, her fingers locate the leather bound book. Before replacing it in the trunk, she shines the

A Pigeon in the Attic

torch on the open page and allows herself a few more minutes to read on.

June 12th. 1962.
Our fifteenth anniversary. We dined at the Majestic. John bought champagne. His deep blue eyes are still the same. When I peer into them, I remember the night we clung together at Amy's bedside and the tears we both shed, when the dawn broke and the fever subsided. He's still handsome to me, but now looks all of his sixty years. The skin round his neck and cheekbones is no longer supple and smooth. His once thick dark hair is now sparse and grey. On occasions, he has been mistaken for my father. My hair is still chestnut brown and as yet my wrinkles don't show.

John gave me an eternity ring, raised his glass and asked if I had any regrets. I can't say we've never had our differences, but no more than most, perhaps less than some couples, more closely matched in age. In some ways the age gap is an advantage. My eagerness for new experiences has kept him young. His wisdom has kept my feet on the ground. Our circle of friends is wider, both older and younger. We entertain and visit the theatre, can afford to travel abroad. Some evenings, we sit by the fireside and read or listen to the radio, content with each other's company - no need to talk. And we still share the pleasure in each other's arms at night. Yes, I could truthfully answer, I have no regrets.

Downstairs Geoffrey is calling her name. Marion replaces the diary and closes the trunk.

Zoe never eats breakfast with her parents. Occasionally she takes a few bites of an apple on her way to the bus stop. Today, however, is different. On the phone in the early hours this morning Colin has sweet-talked her. "It's two days now. You can't keep putting it off," he'd said. "Tomorrow is Saturday. Your father won't be going to work. Maybe he'll listen, not fly off the handle." Zoe doubts it.

Once in the kitchen, Zoe's courage deserts her. She recognizes the signs. Her father, munching muesli, eyes fixed on the Aga, is carefully considering his strategy. But this isn't for his performance in court. It's for her. Is he going to put forward the same old arguments? Or is his plan of campaign to be different? Her mother is fidgeting, rising to top up the teapot, to make more toast neither of them want. At intervals she stares over to her husband.

Zoe searches for a diversion to deflect the attack. "I heard that noise again last night."

Marion is busily buttering. "I had a look in the attic. Thought I heard something, behind the wall, the bit we don't use, but all I found was an old trunk."

"I'll take a look."

"No Geoffrey, it can wait." Marion is staring at her husband willing him to sit down.

"I'll go." Zoe knows that today isn't the day to suggest a meeting with Colin.

Neither parent says anything, just watch their daughter stride through the door and across the hall. When they hear her stomp up the stairs Geoffrey sighs, places his palms on the table and levers himself up to follow her.

"Let her go." Marion brings the unwanted toast to the table. "You know Geoffrey, I've been thinking ... Are we right to stop her if that's what she wants?"

Her husband lowers himself back into the chair and sighs once again. "But it was you, you who was so much against it!"

"I know, but as I said, I've been thinking."

Zoe is relieved to escape to the attic. It takes time for her eyes to adjust to the darkness. In her haste to escape the threats, the pleading, the ultimatum she'd expected from her parents, there was no time to fetch the torch from the garage. Instead, before coming upstairs, she'd hastily felt in her coat pocket and found the personal alarm-cum-flashlight they now give to all students.

She squeezes through the hole with more ease than her mother, then confidently steps from joist to joist. As she squats in the corner, she plays the thin beam of light on the cobwebs that hang from the slates above and the black dust that lies in thick layers below. Nothing here, only the trunk. Curiosity causes her to lift the lid. Her hand brushes silky smooth satin. It is still creamy white, untouched by the grime of the attic. She resists the urge to take it out, in case her fingers leave dark smudges on the flawless material. Instead she lifts the leather bound book. She opens it at a page near the end and holds the light close to decipher the spidery hand.

Oct 10th 1967
John was buried today. He was so looking forward to his retirement - only a few months to go. Mother and father came to the funeral. I couldn't help remembering what they had said all those years ago.

How, with John so much older, I would be left a widow with children to raise on my own. They were right and could have said so, but didn't. Only tried to persuade me to come home. The house is too big for them. They were thinking of selling. If the children and I had the upper floors there would be no need. I said I'd think about it, but how can I leave the cottage that, for twenty years, John and I have called home.

Zoe forgets about looking for the pigeon. She crawls out of the attic, the diary still in her hand. Back in her room she continues to read.

Feb 3rd 1968
Edith was waiting, when we came back here to live. There was a vase of snowdrops in my old bedroom. Mother says, that since she heard the news, Edith hasn't stopped scrubbing and polishing.
I made the decision at Christmas. The cottage held too many memories. Happy memories, but now I must move on. At forty-two, life can't be over. After John died, I went nowhere, except with the children, saw no one but casual acquaintances. Amy is already talking about going away to college. In a few years Lucy will follow or get married. The thought of twenty maybe thirty years on my own is too much to bear.

The wash-house was demolished years ago to make way for a conservatory. The laundry now takes place beneath the worktop in the kitchen. Without the aid of a scrubbing board, mangle or flat iron everything emerges dry and ready to wear in less than two hours.

Zoe is on her knees feeding the automatic washing machine with several pairs of black trousers, skimpy jumpers and undergarments made of next to nothing.

Her mother is unloading the dishwasher. "Did you hear it again last night?"

"Hear what?" Zoe straightens up, nudges the door closed with her knee and clicks the switch to normal wash.

"The pigeon."

"Oh... that... no."

The conversation seems over. Zoe waits to hear the gush of water into the machine then heads for the door.

Her mother calls after her. "I've been talking to your father. Would you like to invite Colin for dinner ... perhaps we could talk about the wedding."

Zoe frowns, unable to believe what she's hearing. 'Oh ... It's all right. I gave the ring back last night. We'll still see each other, but take it slower. Maybe move in together for a while. See if we still feel the same in six months.'

They say the pigeon must have escaped, if it was ever there in the first place. The trunk is now gathering dust, where it has lain for almost forty years. At night, I no longer stand next to the hole in the roof, so the wind flutters my robe.

The thaw has set in. In the garden, rivulets trickle between patches of melting slush. On the roof, a slither becomes a slide, then a dull thud, as snow lands on the patio. It must be getting warmer, although I wouldn't know. Here in the attic I no longer feel the cold, as I did during my lifetime - long ago.

SHOE

Anne Holloway

It's a cold day, rain peeing down. The walk is never pleasant at the best of times. Not much to look at. Paving slabs cracked, leaves drifted in heaps, dog shit lurking beneath so he can't kick through them. Uneven roads mean passing cars spray dirty water up his legs. His bag hurts his shoulder, strap cutting in he's so bony.

The air is grey and the only noise is traffic as it crawls past. You can look into houses if you want, if they don't have those net curtains. A bloke comes out of number 34 and runs to the bus stop. Stupid standing at a bus stop, might as well keep walking. By the time one comes along you're soaked anyway. He walks past the queue of people. Roddy Beck is there, "alright?" they exchange, each with a toss of the head. He'll beat Becky to the gates, he always does.

Stops at the Happy Shopper to buy a carton of milk – he loves milk – ice cold to throw down his gullet as he walks along. Round the corner into the shop, "alright?" asks the girl behind the counter. He raises his eyebrows and throws up his head slightly in reply, chucking the money on the side. Downs the milk, starts running to make up time. Through the gate, bell going. He's beaten Becky, as usual. How come he waits for that bloody bus?

Not a bad day, as days go. Not much aggro, got some work back, did alright. Back out the gate for the walk home.

"Getting the bus, Nealy?"

"Nah, I'll walk." He always walks, they know that. He'll run it, round the back way, takes longer, but the rain has stopped, a bit of sun getting through, naked trees reaching to touch it in case it can spark some leaves off to dress them up again.

Long strides, breathe deep, breathe long, breathe even. Long strides, holding his bag close to stop it banging around. Shit, what's that? He trips, lunges, grabs to stop his fall, but falls anyway. And where his hand went out he feels the heel, curved – pulls his hand back and looks at a shoe. A pantomime shoe, Cinderella's slipper. Small and neat, silver with jewels that catch the weak rays and bounce them back, bright. He casts a glance around, nobody looking, so he puts it in his bag between geography and sports science, first picking off the bits of damp leaf that stick to it.

"'Sthat you?" Who else. She always says it. What would she do if it was someone else? Wouldn't notice most likely. He walks into the front room,

"Alright?" He grunts.

"Alright love. Want some tea?" Said without looking up. She wouldn't make tea, just sit there smoking a fag and watching telly. He puts his hand in his bag, feels the shoe, curls his fingers round it. Turning back to look at her the light from the telly catches her hair and it glows gold and her face looks softer. "Mum..." but then it was gone. He lets go the shoe and climbs the stairs.

Can't face any work tonight, he'll have a bath, stick a pizza in the oven.

"Want a pizza, Mum?" he calls down.

"Mm, okay." She sucks on the fag, lips smacking as she pulls it away, the filter dark brown where she dragged so hard. The ashtray is full, balanced on the arm of the chair. Some bloke has just lost £16,000 because his final answer is wrong.

"Ahh," says Mum.

Under water the sounds are muffled, his hair floats around him like weed in the sea. It is warm in the water and as it cools down he stretches up his foot and twiddles the tap to let more hot in until it slowly splurges out the overflow and he has to get out because there's no more hot to put in.

He forgets the shoe shoved inside his bag until the next morning – walking the usual way – his hand wraps round it again. The sun trickles weakly but the trees seem triumphant, the pavement shiny, the heaps of leaves like fires, he kicks his way through them, revelling in the swish.

"Oi, Becky, why don't you walk?" He shouts at the slumped figure as he passes.

"Alright mate?" to the man at number 34.

"I'm not your fuckin' mate."

On the shop, Happy Shopper – he *is* a happy shopper, round the corner through the door, carton of milk, "good morning," smiling to the girl behind the counter. "Are you takin' the piss?" She glares. He slugs down the milk, white, cold, spilling a bit on his jacket.

Through the gate, beats the bell, beats Becky, starts the day. Gets into trouble, asks too many questions, they're not used to him like this.

"Are you takin' the piss?"

"What's your game?"

"You being funny, boy?"

Shoe

The hall isn't grey it's lilac, the stairs aren't vomit, they're green, French teacher isn't a perve, he's enthusiastic, Granger's not a spas he's just into weird stuff – that's okay.

Not a bad day as days go, bit too much aggro. He walks the usual way home – past the arcade of shops, Pizza panic, Bonus Video, Threshers, Happy Shopper. He looks up the hill behind, a whole sky up there. He takes a run at it, long strides, holding bag, hand on shoe, breathing deep and reaches the top. Spinning around he cries aloud like Tarzan. The sky is huge, town is tiny, grass is soft and dewy, air is clear. He can see his whole life down there – he is alive.

Running home he barges into the front room.

"Mum! Come out for a bit. Mum?" Mum with her golden hair that she has never dyed – used to shine when he was a little kid, who used to laugh before Dad had gone, who used to sing and dance through life, who sits in a chair mostly now, fag in hand, motionless, shineless, songless. He hears the immersion tank gurgling and refilling up in the bathroom and takes the stairs three at a time. She lies in the bath hair streaming like Ophelia, not golden now, but dull. An empty strip of pills lying on the floor. He uncurls his fingers from the muddy old shoe and drops it to the floor. He kneels beside her and wonders if he should lift her out before she gets cold and wrinkled but instead leans forward and turns on the tap to let in a little more hot.

DON'T DO VOODOO

Toby Malamute

From all the tossing and turning the polystyrene was turning her skin red. She felt like someone was watching her. Either through the doorway, eyes around the frame, or through the window. But if she drew the curtains it was too dark and it scared her.

Bed sheets never seemed like a necessity. But now she wanted one. They were in the middle of a heat wave and the polystyrene sheet didn't absorb sweat, it just formed a sticky uncomfortable layer between her and unconsciousness. And she got up. Pulled on the thinnest clothes she could find. They were all black and she walked to the door.

The street burned even at that time of night and cars streamed by her, their lights forming trails in the air. People merged into a faceless mass of sound and smell and she knew she was not one of them. The heat of the bodies around her made her skin prickle where the polystyrene had rubbed her. She put her head down and got through it. On the street where the shop was there was no one around.

The door was never locked and inside the shelves were filled with voodoo paraphernalia and contraptions for which she did not know the use. She pressed a bell on the counter and a voice croaked from behind the thick curtains that covered the back wall. "Enter."

She pulled the curtain back and there a woman in a shawl sat at a table with a large candle in the centre. She sat down opposite her, the chair was uncomfortable.

"Are you sure this is what you want Cindy?" the woman asked her.

"I'm sure, I fear him, he's insane, I know he's watching me."

"He is, but are you sure you would not like to handle this another way? It won't be pretty."

"I'm sure," Cindy leant around the candle so she was closer to the woman, who looked in her thirties, but had grey hair and Cindy knew she was in her sixties, "he just won't leave me alone."

"Then look into the flame, and I shall get the doll."

In his heart the candle burned. It grew smaller as time went by but gave just the same amount of light. He knew that when it burned out, it would leave a puddle of wax almost as heavy as the candle was when it was new, but it could no longer burn, only form itself into something solid. Still it could be malleable, but the heat he had now was the best way to form the shape of his destiny. He knew that the burning was telling him to act, and he must act before the passion burnt out.

The light from the candle was brighter at night. He had been trying to define it since it began to burn brighter than normal at two a.m. Now the dawn light was creeping in. He took a deep breath, put on his favourite hat and walked towards the door.

"Hot dog!" he said to the salesman. "You are completely getting me."

"I knew exactly what you wanted the minute you walked in. A man of your..." the salesman wanted to say stature or style but the man's body was unusually long and his elbows stuck out at strange angles, plus he wore a sports jacket with padded shoulders and a lime green trilby. Instead he looked for a discerning feature and settled on facial hair. "A man of your beard would want a pink Cadillac."

"Just show me where to sign, I need it, it just says *love* to me."

Apparently as long as the credit card is valid your signature can be whatever you like, even if it's dumb. The man wrote "LARRY", in big letters on every bit of paper and grinned like the cat that got the cream.

With a wide friendly wave Larry pulled off the forecourt. The car was brand new so he treated it gently, cruising along at twenty-five mph for the first few blocks and picking all the leafiest avenues. The sun was shining and the birds were singing and Larry waved at everybody on the way home, even though he knew none of them.

"Good morning ma'am," he called to a woman with a baby in a stroller, "I bought this for my honey." He parped the horn and the baby began to cry. The nanny looked unsure of what to make of the situation.

There were a few stops to be made before he could go home, first the bakery. He dropped by and picked up ten baked Alaskan Tarts, her favourite. Next was the florist where he procured thirty red red roses, all as sweet as the autumn morning. The third stop was the masterstroke, "my piss de resistance," Larry thought to himself.

By noon Larry was cruising back along the highway at forty-five in the fast lane, the Cadillac as fragrant and tasty as the woman herself and towing forty-five red love-heart balloons from its wing mirrors and bumpers.

"Smooth," he thought.

In the heat of the afternoon her thoughts drifted like the smoke of her cigarette. Cindy had no money for furniture yet, so lay on the sticky polystyrene. She liked the house much better in the day and was just happy to be away from him.

Their three years together had been sinister. He would always be doing something she couldn't comprehend. Like coming home with a cat in a box and expecting her to look after it. She hated cats and whenever it scratched her she would make a mental note against him, more bitterness with highlights of resentment.

He held her back and sucked their resources into wild schemes that came to nothing, and ended with bad people coming to her door. He was gullible and easily-led; his influence over the world he lived in was confined to wild bursts of spending on random items, most of them useless, if not illegal. What was she to do with a box of stolen caviar or a magnum of dusty champagne that used to sit in the wine rack of one of Larry's 'clients'?

Although he lived on the other side of town in their old house, Larry was more often than not pulling up on the driveway of her house at the very top of the cliff road, and making a scene at the door. She had gone to great pains to move as far away as was possible. But still he brought the gifts.

"Why," she thought, "would he think a poodle was better than a cat?" Cindy had made him take it back. Like the bird's nest soup and oysters, and the string quartet playing 'Lady in Red'.

It was possible the woman in the shop knitted the dolls herself. This one had elbows that stuck out at strange angles and a little green hat. Cindy cradled it in her arms and it gave her the security of her first cuddly toy, Finsbury, that was a little girl in a little red dress and she loved it to that day. Finsbury was at her mum's house, all the way over on the other coast. In Cindy's financial state Finsbury seemed more like a million miles away.

Now she only had the voodoo doll for comfort and at one o'clock she heard the familiar and regular sound of a car pulling onto her driveway. She wasn't going to get up until he started hammering on the door.

Which he did, in less than a minute's time. And when he started he wouldn't stop until she answered him. "Cindy! Cindy! Come out here," he called, banging on the door monotonously, "Cindy Cindy, come out here, I love ya!"

At first she had made sure she was out, but no matter how late she returned, he would still be there, waiting. Uncharacteristically the knocking at the door ceased. There was a short pause, and then a burst of loud Dixie-town jazz erupted from outside and the knocking resumed. The music was deafening and holding the doll tight Cindy went to open the door.

"Look what I brung ya!" shouted Larry over the music.

"You fucking moron," said Cindy.

"But come look." Larry was not deterred, "I got you all your favourites, and balloons, just look at those balloons."

"Fuck off Larry, can't you just leave me alone?"

"I can't leave you alone darling, I love ya." His eyes bulged as he said it.

"Please Larry, you need to move on." She'd said it a hundred times but she thought she owed him one more try before she took drastic action. "You have to leave me alone or I can't move forward and achieve anything. You're holding me back like you always have. You can be happy if you let go and do whatever the hell it is that you're doing, just, without me."

Larry stared at Cindy blankly.

"Come and check out the upholstery honey," he said. "It's real plush inside."

It was clear to Larry that Cindy loved the car, she was not yelling or throwing anything at him this time. He knew that if he could just get her to sit in the driver's seat she would fall in love with it and by consequence, him. He was there, the time was that afternoon on Cindy's driveway, and he was the man, he was Larry.

He waved his fists in the air in time to the Dixie beat to try and woo her towards the car. She held up a little doll in front of him.

"I got you a gift in return," she said, and Larry was so pleased at that moment, he felt like doing a twirl on the spot and getting down on one knee.

Cindy gave the right foot of the doll a sharp twist. And Larry's right foot shot out to the side and stayed there.

Larry looked at his foot.

Cindy let go of the right foot and took hold of the left, and Larry's left foot shot out to the side. She went back to the right, and then the left. And somehow Larry kept time with the music and co-ordinated the fist waving with the foot kicking. He felt cool.

"I'm dancin' for ya honey and I just can't stop," he called and grinned, gesturing towards the Cadillac.

It was clear that Cindy had never used a voodoo doll before. She twisted the limbs as hard as she could but only succeeded in making Larry throw his arms and legs out in different directions. She was making him dance and she threw the doll on the floor.

Larry executed a perfect spin to the side and danced back in front of her. Cindy realised she was going to have to get tough.

Inside the house Cindy rifled through her still half packed belongings until she found her sewing kit. She took from it three long thick needles and went back to the door.

When she got there Larry had picked up the voodoo doll and was playing with it. He spasmed and twitched as he contorted it. After a couple of minutes he seemed able to make his feet keep time with the music using the doll and tried to spice it up by twisting the waist and making his hips gyrate.

"Excuse me," said Cindy and snatched the doll back from him.

And with no further ceremony, she pushed one of the needles through his knee.

Larry let out a loud yelp and fell to the floor. The yelp alerted the attention of Mr Johnson, who was mowing the lawn opposite.

"That man's a menace to society!" he shouted over the sound of the mower.

"I know," called Cindy back and placed the doll at the top of the drive.

She rolled it and Larry followed suit, rolling down towards the car. Cindy picked up the doll and opened the car door. She yanked Larry to his feet and frog-marched him to the Cadillac. Cindy was getting good at manipulating the doll and she positioned Larry in the driver's seat and slammed the door.

"Now," she said and popped one of the balloons with a needle, "if I ever see you back here again I'm going to walk you off that cliff." She pointed to the railings that protected the road from the sheer drop.

"But," Larry sputtered, "but I love ya!" He grinned dopily, "I brung ya chocolates, and flowers and the car and balloons, just look at those balloons."

Cindy shrieked, and it took all her concentration but she managed to manipulate the doll delicately enough to make Larry take the handbrake off and the Pink Cadillac with its swarm of bobbing hearts, rolled slowly backwards off the drive and down the road.

"I love ya!" called Larry, and he put his foot on the brake and turned the wheel back towards the house. Before he could start the engine Cindy pushed a needle through each of his sticky-out elbows. She yanked his foot off the break and the car started backwards again gathering speed. She figured the guardrail to the cliff would stop the car.

But she was wrong. The Cadillac broke straight through the thin metal and plopped over the edge.

"I loooooooooove yaaaaaaaaaaaaaaaaaaaaaaaaaaaaaaaaaaaaa!" screamed Larry.

Cindy stared at the cliff in disbelief.

"Good riddance," Mr Johnson called across and returned to his mowing.

"Sure," said Cindy and looked around, embarrassed, before hiding the doll under her sweatshirt and going back inside.

She decided a nap might be nice in the afternoon sun, yes a nap, the heat would surely have dried the polystyrene by then. And Cindy curled up with the doll in her arms on the scratchy surface, finally able to find peaceful sleep.

THE MAD MAN IN THE ATTIC

Louise Slocombe

"I have no idea how long he's been up there," I said. "Days, weeks, months even. Who knows?"

"He must have been very quiet," the policewoman said, raising her eyebrows at her colleague across the table. "You'd think you would hear the floorboards creaking in an old house like this."

It's really saying something when the police can make you feel stupid.

"I don't spend much time upstairs," I said. I don't like it up there. Too quiet. Too many empty rooms. Most evenings I'm slumped in the living room, TV controller in one hand, whisky glass in the other. I don't always make it up to bed. It's not really so surprising that I never heard him. And he could have watched me easily enough. When he heard the front door slam, he could have peered through one of the grimy little attic windows, and seen me striding down the drive, or reversing out in the car, scraping that bloody gatepost on the way, and he would have known that the coast was clear.

"But you must have had a sense that you weren't alone, surely? A feeling that you were being watched?" Amanda at work had shuddered in horror when I told her during a fag break. I told her not to tell anyone else. I didn't want the whole office knowing stuff about me.

"I can't say I did," I said. To tell the truth, I often feel watched in that house. Too many memories.

"But don't you feel violated?" she asked. "Knowing that someone was there all that time, looking through your things?"

"No," I said, stubbing out my fag in the little metal bin they provide for us. "I don't really." Liberated, I wanted to say, I feel liberated, but I didn't think she would understand. I wasn't sure I understood myself.

My sister was appalled. "Anything could have happened to you, Ali, he could have sneaked down with an axe, he could have set your house on fire at night and burnt you alive in your bed. It's that area you live in, it's really going downhill."

"It could have happened anywhere," I said. "He could have picked on any house, anywhere."

The Mad Man in the Attic

She gave me a hard stare. "I don't think so. That huge house, only one car in the drive, a woman on her own coming and going. You're an easy target, Ali. I know I've said all this before however many times, but you really should think about moving. I know you're attached to the place and all of that, but you can't afford to maintain it, you don't even use most of the rooms. I can't think Geoff would have wanted you to be living like this, moping around in there all alone, not changing anything."

Tact is not my sister's strong point.

"And you could sell it for a fortune," she went on, "to some landlord wanting to rent to students. You could cram I don't know how many students into that place."

"I know, I know," I said. I did know. I'd been checking out prices in the property guide.

It was Sammy from next door who saw him. He'd been going on about cutting the hedge at the side for ages and I'd finally given in. Apparently there's a law now about fifteen foot hedges, or so he says.

"Didn't know you had a lodger," he said, when I came back from work. He'd been hanging around, checking the hedge with a spirit level, making sure there wasn't a leaf out of place. If I'd left him to it for long enough, he would probably have started making topiary animals along the top.

"I haven't," I said.

"Oh," he said, "that's strange."

"What's strange, Sammy?" Sammy's nice enough, but I can't be doing with neighbourly small talk. All I was thinking about was getting inside and unwinding with a nice glass of red wine.

"It's just I saw someone coming out of that little door up there in your roof and going down your fire escape."

My stomach lurched. "Someone going down the fire escape? Oh my God! Are you sure?"

"Quite sure," he said. "A little old man, he looked like, all hunched over. Wearing lots of clothes. He looked a bit ... well, sort of down and out, I'd say."

"Shit," I said. "What the hell's going on?"

"He didn't look like a burglar," Sammy said. "He wasn't carrying anything. Tell you what, do you want me to come in and help you check it out?"

In my flustered state I nearly agreed. Then I collected myself. I wasn't having Sammy in the house nosing around. For a second, I almost wondered if he'd made it up to give him an excuse to get through my front door. I mean, what a stupid bloody thing to say, "didn't know you had a lodger". As if a lodger would use the fire escape.

I didn't want to go in, but Sammy was watching so I had to. In the kitchen, I poured myself that glass of wine. My breath was coming in short gasps and my face felt weirdly stretched, like I was wearing a mask. I picked up the bread knife, although God knows what I would have done with it, and went round the downstairs rooms. Nothing seemed to have been disturbed. Well to me it didn't. Anyone else might think there'd been a team of burglars in there, the state it's all in. After that, I took a deep breath and went upstairs, my heart thumping in my ears. I went in all the rooms one by one, holding the bread knife out in front of me, looking behind the doors. No footprints in the dust. That left the attic. I went back downstairs and poured myself a brandy this time. I downed it in one gulp, came back up and went over to the door at the bottom of the attic stairs. It was still locked, the key sitting in the keyhole. I turned it as quietly as I could and slowly opened the door. It occurred to me that he could have come back up the fire escape while I was in the house.

I snapped on the light at the bottom of the stairs. The only sound was a bird chirping up on the roof. I went up the stairs slowly, holding my breath, feeling light headed from suspense and alcohol. It was cold up here. I reached the top of the stairs, stopped short and screamed. I'd never heard myself scream before. Then I stood there, gasping like a fish.

The attic had been rearranged. Normally you can only walk a few feet into the room before your way is blocked by piles of cardboard boxes, bulging bin bags, bits of old furniture, all left where I've dumped them. But now, things were neatly stacked against the walls and you could see from one end of the attic to the other. But it wasn't just that. The whole of the attic had been laid out, using my old junk, in kind of displays, like some weird art gallery or museum. Facing me, on a drunkenly lopsided armchair with worn floral covers, was my big teddy, wearing my wedding dress, one eye coyly covered by the veil. Leading away from the armchair, a pathway had been set out, lined with books leaning sideways like toppled dominoes. I followed it, fascinated. In one place, a file of student essays had been taken apart and folded into origami shapes, in another, the rooms of a dolls house were filled with seashells. I recognised stuff we had dumped up here when Geoff and I first got the house, grimy fake chandeliers arranged so they were reflected endlessly in carefully angled tarnished mirrors. There were things I took when we cleared out my parents' house, stuff

I had loved as a child like the big patterned glass fish that used to sit on the windowsill in the toilet and my Dad's painting-by-numbers of gypsy flamenco dancers. Geoff had deemed them too hideous to be on show. Zigzagging crazily between the sloping ceilings was a long clothes line hung with things I used to wear in my partying days, glittery frocks, tarnished diamante necklaces, a pink feather boa fluttering in the draught from the windows.

At the end of the book-lined path, there were photographs laid out flat on the floor forming a huge spiral. They were held down neatly at the corners with the china animals I used to collect as a child. The photographs were all of me. They were arranged more or less chronologically, starting with a black and white photo of me as a chubby baby wrapped in a crocheted shawl, watched over by two porcelain hippos and a tortoise with a compass set into its shell. Then there were school portraits, with and without braces on my teeth, holiday snaps with my family on the windswept beach at Scarborough and a graduation photo where I was grinning inanely, clutching my degree. After the wedding pictures, there were snaps from ten, twenty years ago, me laughing with friends at a party, me and Geoff on top of the Eiffel Tower, me toasting my parents at their silver wedding. In the centre of the spiral, held down by a mouse balancing on an ear of corn and a trumpeting elephant, was a picture of me hugging Geoff on top of a mountain, blue skies behind us. I stood and stared at them all. It felt as if I was looking at someone I had known a very long time ago and hadn't seen for years.

In a corner of the attic was a little campsite. My tent was thrown over two stacks of cardboard boxes and my sleeping bag was rolled out inside it, along with the plastic plates and cutlery I used to use for camping. There were a few packets of sandwiches and a crushed box of cakes in the corner. The sleeping bag was a bit smelly.

I walked slowly back through the attic, feeling disoriented. At the top of the stairs I paused at the teddy bear in the wedding dress. Its arms were outstretched as if in greeting. I remembered carrying that bear around with me everywhere as a child.

After that, I did what anyone else would have done. I went downstairs and I called the police. They came and looked in the attic. I wouldn't let them touch anything. They made a few calls and then some other people came. These people were from some kind of home. They knew who he was, they were joking about it. The police left and the people from the home sat in their car, waiting in the driveway. It was an ordinary saloon car, so he didn't seem to be considered dangerous. I stayed in the house feeling uncomfortable, watching out of the window. He turned up eventually, just as it was getting dark. He was small and bent, like Sammy said, swathed up in dark clothes, carrying a couple of plastic bags. There was no struggle. He got into the car and they started up the engine. I had this sudden urge to go out there, to introduce myself to him. I wanted to thank him but I didn't know what for. Taking an interest in me perhaps. I went over to the door, but in the end I just stood there, watching the red tail-lights through the glass as they disappeared down the drive.

PILLOW TALK

Ian Douglas

http://www.pillowtalk.com

Welcome to Pillow Talk

By entering Pillow Talk you agree to our Terms of Use.

If you wish to review these terms, then **Click Here.**

| I agree | I disagree |

Entering Pillow Talk.

MAIN MENU

Pillow Talk Home page
Pillow Talk Personals
Pillow Talk Chat
Pillow Talk Messages
Pillow Talk Babes

For the chat room **click here.**

Please wait while the applet loads.

Enter

Selecting pussy room.

There is one person in the pussy room.

stud_boy. Profile: 31, young exec type, always up for it.

hotlips has entered the pussy room.
 Profile: 27, swf, ok looking, serious offers only!

stud_boy: howdy there little mama.
hotlips: hi stud_boy, u busy?
stud_boy: no way Jose, how's it hanging?
hotlips: oh u know, same old stuff and u?
stud_boy: i'm cool, u home alone tonight?
hotlips: yep, how about u.
stud_boy: ditto, u looking for action?
hotlips: sure am, feeling hot?
stud_boy: hotter than July and gagging for it.
hotlips: great! cyber ?
stud_boy: u said the magic words sweet-cakes. cam-to-cam?
hotlips: lol. too shy. just cyber OK?
stud_boy: no problemo, cyber is cool. stats?
hotlips: 27yo/180cms/65k. real wet. u?
stud_boy: 31yo/189cms/75k 9" uncut.
hotlips: wow! u are burning me up, u like it real dirty?
stud_boy: keep it cumming babe,
hotlips: sure? full on?
stud_boy: yes please sweetie! u into 69?
stud_boy: still there babe?
hotlips: can i ask a question?
stud_boy: as long as it's dirty.
hotlips: do u ever get lonely?
stud_boy: that's not dirty, cum on, talk dirty to me.
hotlips: no really, are u lonely.
stud_boy: look no time wasters OK?
hotlips: no really, i know i'm lonely, are u?
stud_boy: ok fuck off then slut.
stud_boy has left the chat room.
There is one person in the pussy room.

LETTER OF THE LAW

Loay Hady

My increased knowledge of the world's laws all started in Hong Kong. My then wife found out about my bit on the side so I had to quickly move on, as there she was allowed to kill me for my infidelity, so long as she carried out the murder with her bare hands. I didn't have much money or time so when I got to the airport I caught the next available short haul flight. I ended up in Indonesia and got a job scraping gum off peoples shoes, the work was ok, but having lost my wife and my mistress, I was going to have to see to myself for a while, but it wasn't worth the risk here... the penalty for masturbation was decapitation. I had to get me another wife so as soon as I'd saved up enough, I headed out to Saudi Arabia where local custom allowed me to have up to four, I landed me the most beautiful belly dancer in the whole harem and for our honeymoon we headed out to Florida. While I enjoyed Disneyland, I wasn't overly satisfied with the sex. It became stale after a few days, as the only permissible position within this state was the missionary.

My wife did like America though and asked if we could stay for a while touring, so I figured cool, why not... we headed out to Gary in Indiana, where we found one of the nicest pizza parlours I'd ever been to. The pizzas were great but the garlic bread was even better. We wanted to round off one evening with a film, but unfortunately local law forbade us from going in to the cinema within four hours of eating garlic. It wasn't all bad though; we headed back to the hotel where the culmination of a massive row ended with some kinky make-up sex, I was surprised to find she loved me talking dirty.

All was well with our newfound foul-mouthed sex life till money ran low and I had to find work. I got offered a job in Willowdale, Oregon testing pillows, and though the money was good, she was the one no longer impressed with our sex life, as in Willowdale it's decreed that no man may curse while having sex with his wife.

She stuck with me for four days before disappearing. The note said she was going to start a new life in Utah. I tried to stick out the pillow testing job, but began to worry that all the lying down would mean my muscles would atrophy, so I decided to head to Utah and track my wife down.

When I eventually caught up with her, I found her in the middle of the street, smoking a crack pipe, eating stolen caviar and playing football with a hamster she'd kicked to death. To make matters worse a policeman wandered up just a few moments after I got there. She was screwed. I figured I should just leave her, head back to Saudi and get another wife (two down two to go) but the police officer turned to me and asked if I was this woman's husband, I replied in the affirmative thinking nothing of it, to which the policeman replied,

"In that case sir, I'm arresting you for taking a class A drug in public, stealing caviar and kicking an animal to death." I thought he was joking and explained I hadn't done any of those things. He said he was well aware of that fact, but in Utah a husband is responsible for every criminal act committed by his wife in his presence.

Luckily a robbery ensued across the street and the policeman had to prioritise that, so I grabbed my wife and headed to the nearest Hertz. I rented a car and headed to Los Angeles. I was still mad at my wife for leaving me. I wanted to hurt her the way she had hurt me, and I'd chosen the right place to do so. In LA a man is legally entitled to beat his wife with a leather belt or strap, but the belt can't be wider than two inches, unless he has his wife's consent to beat her with a wider strap. I only had a four-inch wide belt, but I did have her consent to use it. I was feeling quite de-stressed after administering the lashing so I thought I'd go for a walk. A wiry fellow with an elephant asked if I wouldn't mind taking his elephant for a walk down the street in exchange for three hundred dollars, as he urgently needed to attend a yoga class.

I argued that surely I wasn't allowed to walk an elephant down a busy street, but apparently it was fine... as long as I held on to its lead. I took the lead and the discussed figure and headed down town. Half way through my stroll I saw a rare Barry Manilow B-side for sale in a retro record shop window, I was beside myself with joy, unfortunately though, the sign on the door said no pets, so I couldn't take him in with me.

Fortunately, a kind mono-browed man walked up to me and asked me if I was looking for somewhere to leave my elephant. I was surprised but I replied, "indeed I am." To which he said "I know how you feel, dude. No worries though. You're allowed to park it in a car parking bay, but it's subject to the same hourly tariffs." What a stroke of luck. I tied him to the meter and went to buy the record but ended up spending six hours in the store on account of their great selection. When I left to get my elephant, I found that it had been clamped as I'd only paid for half an hour. Fearing the yoga man's wrath when he found his elephant in the restrictive yellow footwear, I figured it was time to head back to Blighty.

The Letter of the Law

I grabbed my healing wife and caught the next flight home, which was truly shocking. Turbulence was incessant and I wasn't allowed a cigarette so naturally when I touched down in York airport I was more than a little antsy. I needed to destroy something, I headed to the nearest archery shop and bought myself a bow and arrow and wandered the streets looking for a Scotsman to shoot, which is as we all know is perfectly legal. Having found a suitably kilted candidate, I got him into my sights and was just about to let fly, when he started to shake his head and smile, "not today you're not, pal, it's Sunday." Damn, the cheeky git was right, Sunday was the only day such an act was *illegal*. I shot anyway, and as the arrow flew into his shoulder and he crashed into a heap, I decided I would tell the court I was still on U.S. time. Maybe there was a law for that too.

UNTITLED

Emma O'Brien

Try choosing the theme song to a film of your life. Not as easy as it looks. You could just use your favourite, but I think that'd be a bit of a cop out. Your life might not necessarily fit in with it. In fact, I'm going to be honest for a minute. I don't know why this is even one of the set questions. I only chose it because it looked more interesting than the poetry one. I'm not sure exactly how interesting a biopic of a Year 11 in a scabby suburban school would be, or why the soundtrack would make thrilling reading.

Maybe the fact that mine's a total mess would make it a bit more interesting. I have no desire to answer this question or any of the others, but I'm going to keep writing because I know you're going to watch me like a hawk for the rest of the lesson in case I run out of the room and do something silly again. I wouldn't worry though. The psychiatrist's report says I'm fine. Mind you, there's a lot they don't know.

I don't think there is a song about what's going on in my head these days. Sarah Matthews used to write songs. Remember her? I know you never taught her, but you'll have been warned about me before I came back, and probably you heard everything that was said while I was away. Whatever you've heard, I can promise you, you really don't know anything about her. But she loved writing songs. In fact the first time I ever met her was at dinnertime when she was looking for the music room. She had her guitar with her, on her first day and everything. Very dedicated.

Maybe I could find some soundtrack songs there. There must be thousands of songs about how things could have turned out differently, and that's pretty appropriate. The problem I have is that after everything that's happened I'm still not sure if I would have wanted it to turn out any differently.

I remember the first day Sarah was here pretty well, considering it was a year ago. She used to get the kind of funny looks that I get now. Not for the same reason though; it was only when she spoke. She was Welsh. (Mistake with my tenses there- she still is, wherever she might have gone now). Oh, and just to confirm your views on Amy Mullaine, we first saw Sarah while we were trying to break into the art room. I'm going to be rude and blame you, because we'd been telling you for weeks it was too cold in the drama class to rehearse our set piece.

Amy was never that keen on Sarah, so you have to give her at least some credit for having better judgement than me. You're right about Ames being a bit superficial though. I'm her best friend so I can say it, but she has this annoying little habit of picking out one tiny thing about a person, even if she really likes them. She did that with Sarah's front tooth, because it was grey. If I liked Amy less I suppose I could generalize and blame her for a lot that went on with me and Sarah, because she got me to ask about the tooth. I'll be honest and say I'd wondered about it as well, even knowing it was trivial. So I asked her why it was grey.

I'll record that conversation for you because I know you like natural dialogue:

"My tooth? What about it?"

She looked at me like I was nuts for even thinking about it, which I feel is slightly harsh as after all not everyone has a grey front tooth.

"Well - it's grey. Unlike the rest of them."

"And what?"

"And nothing, I only said, what happened to it?"

"Forehead," she said, smirking at me, then rolling over onto her side (we were sitting on my bed doing Maths coursework at the time),

"You what?"

"You know that game, the one you play in juniors where you basically split into teams and run at each other?"

I had to think about that for a minute. "What, British Bulldog?"

"Yeah, that's it. So I was playing that and I smacked into this kid. He got concussion. I got a dead tooth."

"Who lost then?"

She laughed. I think she enjoyed telling that story. I wonder if it turned out the same every time she did.

"Well, he got a scar. But then again some people like scars. Think it makes someone look more interesting."

"I've always gone for grey teeth myself."

That might sound like a subtle line but I really had no idea I wasn't joking until she flipped onto her other side and kissed me.

(If you're still reading this I so wish I was there to see your face).

The thing about kissing is it's never like it is in films where it all just goes nice and smoothly. I don't know if it gets better as you get older but in my limited experience there's always lip biting or tooth clicking. And that was the weird thing about it, and it's bothered me ever since, that time it wasn't crappy. It was like film kissing. And it was only that once. I kissed her God knows how many times after that (isn't it scandalous! I'm such a dirty lesbian, and me predicted six A's as well) and it was always normal in that slightly wrong sort of way.

Or maybe I'm just remembering it wrong, who knows. Thing is, I remember deciding right off the bat there was no way I was going to tell anyone (not even Amy, and I know you wonder what we always find to talk about) but I could just hear Amy asking if grey teeth tasted any different. I know the rest of that night I spent trying to think of a really clever way to answer that question, even though I knew I'd never be asked, just to keep me from thinking about Sarah because I wasn't sure I wanted to go there.

Do you know what? I don't care if you are still reading this. I think I've pretty much failed the mock anyway, so why don't I just carry on getting all this off my chest? It's been there too long. I love the way you're all happy to stare at me and talk to me in that we-are-here-to-help-you tone without actually mentioning anything, so why don't I tell you straight? Even now, I'm not sorry. Even after what she did to me (and that hurt, not that anyone much seems to care about that) I think I'd probably do the whole thing again, all six months of it, if she came in the door now. I never thought long term when we were together (and I've never called it that before, not even in my head) but if I'm honest I never saw an end to it either. That was stupid of me. Nothing like that's destined to last, is it?

But I miss Sarah. I hate her in a lot of ways, and I never mention her any more, but I miss her.

You'll probably like this actually. One of the things I really miss is going to her house, because they had a bookcase in the bathroom. I thought that was brilliant. Nobody in my house reads except for me and all my books are stashed in a bread crate under my bed. Remember that time at parent's evening you told my mum she should extend my reading material? She got really wound up about that. When we got home I had to listen to a half an hour lecture about getting above myself. Thanks, by the way.

I loved that bookcase, it was just such a random place to keep one, and it didn't have novels on it, they were textbook sort of things. Sarah wasn't too fond of it, I don't think. She certainly didn't have much time for me bouncing back downstairs to tell her all about how great it was.

Another conversation, just because it's going round my head now:
Sarah when I asked her about the bookshelf (not looking at me):
"It's work stuff."
"In the toilet?"
She looked really offended. I was upset about that because I wasn't ripping it, I loved it. She had this really snappy way of

answering when she was offended, and it didn't suit her Welshness.

"Mam and Dad are psychologists, so they get all these research journals and stuff. They have to keep current things and it clutters up the house."

I couldn't work out if she thought I was an ignorant pleb or she was embarrassed by her parents' job. Looking back I think the first option's more likely. I mean my mum does three days a week in Asda. I wouldn't be embarrassed by that, never mind saying she did something like psychology. I bet Sarah's parents are upset with her though. I mean God knows what you must think of me now, if you haven't chucked my paper in the bin. Imagine how my mum and dad feel. And how Sarah's nice posh doctor parents must have felt. It's not bad enough that her little brother was always getting suspended for something (seven months Sarah was here and Rich never even got to start, they wouldn't let him in. Maybe you've seen the files on hopeless cases, I don't know), but then your nice clever daughter who's been entered for Higher Maths starts pulling random scruffy girls. I suppose it's like me getting caught robbing sweets out of my mum's Asda, only worse.

Not that I've got anything against getting off with people of the same sex, obviously. Not that I'd be in a position to comment if I did. For a start, I know about half of our year have been caught shoplifting and I seem to be the only one who's tried to top herself, so maybe I'd have been better off nicking out of Superdrug than getting up to lesbianism at weekends. Funnily enough, my parents were more sympathetic than Sarah's, and my parents did nothing but scream at me for two days and ignore me for a week after I got out of hospital. Her parents came round and had a go at my mum and dad about how upset and disrupted she was by everything and how they hoped they'd keep me under better control in the future.

My dad threw them out, which I liked. I cried, actually, because I heard him telling them how I wasn't evil and corrupting and whatever else as they went, and I hadn't heard a nice word about myself for days. That sounds like a load of self pity, but I really don't blame anyone for being angry or thinking I'm stupid after what I did. You said yourself on my last report, Natalie is generally very mature. Tipping the medicine box down your throat is a lot of things, but mature isn't really one of them. If I'd meant to die that would have been different, but I don't know what I meant to do. Make Sarah sorry, or keep myself out of all the shit that was about to hit the fan. The most common accusation I've had is attention seeking, but really, I think that's too nice a way of putting it, because for that I would have had to have been thinking about other people, and I know I wasn't. I just couldn't handle what Sarah did.

Admittedly, she didn't start it, but you probably only heard about the bit after the canteen. Just in case you didn't, I'll tell you. At least someone might understand why I acted like such an idiot. It was acting like an idiot that made it happen. We used to hide in the music rooms. The little practice rooms in the arts block with the little windows on the door. Someone must have seen us, I suspect Stephen Bailey but that's between us. I can't think of anyone else who could have got from there to the right desk in the science room to leave that note for my next lesson.

And as soon as I saw it I knew that wasn't it. I thought people were looking at me funny on the way up, you know the way your stomach goes when something bad's about to happen? I was shaking when I sat down, and I dropped the note on the floor. As soon as I saw it I got up and legged it downstairs but the last thing I saw was someone picking it up, so there went the last of them, if they hadn't heard already.

I never thought I'd like the staggered dinnertimes at this school but at least I knew where to find Sarah. The stupid thing was I wasn't even thinking about myself, I just wanted to find her and tell her before someone else did.

Sadly they already had. And she decided to erase me. I stood right in front of her and she just turned her back on me. I remember shouting at her, and then Amy turning up and trying to drag me back to science, and one of the dinner ladies shouting at her for shouting at Sarah. I just left. I ran home. Amy followed me for a while, but I was on my own when I got back.

My sister says I'd left the front door open (remember Beth?) which was what made next door come over and that's how they found me. I'd fainted by then but the hospital said that wasn't the tablets. They were those pink ibuprofen that look like Smarties. I used to love the taste, couldn't touch one now. I remember throwing them all up, but I'm not sure if that was the hospital or the ambulance. God, it feels like ten years ago and it hasn't been a month.

I'm sorry, I don't know why I wrote all this. I don't know anything, maybe that's why. I don't know where Sarah is, I don't know if Amy or my family will forgive me, I don't know if I'm "still a dyke" as some Year Eights put it this morning. And even after everything I don't know if I care.

In conclusion, the life of Natalie Chapman would be a silent film, because she's sick of all the noise.

PHOTOGRAPHS

Frances Thimann

Anna David returns to her mother's house after the old lady's sudden death in hospital. Even though their relationship had not always been an easy one, Anna is nevertheless in shock and grief. She finds some diversion and consolation, however, in looking through the family photographs...

I took down the shabby, old-fashioned albums from the shelf. I knew that these too, like all my mother's documents and letters, would be carefully arranged, firmly labelled, though her handwriting had become a little unsteadier in the last few years.

These days, perhaps, families do not record their lives in this way. I do not know if modern ways are better, but for me there was some comfort, some enchantment even in those old, fading photographs. And I thought that somehow, by studying these pictures of her life and her family, I might become closer to my mother. I hoped that in this way, even at this stage, I might understand her more clearly, without the tensions and the unhappiness that had occurred so often between us through the years.

I sat that evening in the little study with the albums strewn all about me, and the stiff covers opened to the past.

Yes - here was a picture that I remembered still, a very early one; my mother, Miriam, as a baby, lying on her mother's lap in long elaborate clothing, exotic like a pagan princess glimpsed in some old travel book. Her face was small and dark, intense even then. She was the youngest child of five, the only girl, and several years younger than her brothers, very much loved. Even as a baby she was beautiful, even as a young girl she would have become used to receiving admiration. I looked at the picture for a long time; that early likeness seemed to explain so much to me. There were many others, simple family records - my mother in a great old-fashioned pram like a Viking ship sailing across a modest suburban garden; unforgiving school uniforms as she grew up, harsh haircuts. Family groups in porches in outdated clothes, hats like acorns; on beaches in flapping absurd bathing costumes.

Going to work, her first day perhaps, a secretary in the family firm. A plain winter coat and a beret, topped with its rakish slanted twig, as if she might be lifted up and placed in a more enticing world. She faces the camera, and the adventure of earning her living: excited, calm.

I put the album down for a moment. I wondered what she might have wanted from her life then. Her family had been modest, they could not afford an education for her. For most women at that time there was no prospect of excitement or fulfilment, only marriage and maternity. Her working life would be short-lived, often dull.

Did she find fulfilment or excitement with my father, with her children?

I took up the second album. I found a likeness of my father as her suitor, bespectacled and plain even as a young man, soon to be a professor; she would have respected his knowledge, his scholarship. A studio portrait of Miriam on her engagement, her dark, challenging eyes seeming to look a little apart here, as if recently alerted to something of wider import, or to encompass more of the world; lovely as a film star, but innocent, without glamour or self-awareness. A folder of their wedding photos, my father seeming nervous and uncomfortable, finding himself for once a centre of attention. My mother radiant, her long slender-fitting dress circling suddenly wide about her feet, as if showing the fulfilment that a bride should find in marriage.

The young mother with her new baby, joy cut deep and dark in every line and angle of her face: my sister Lucy, lovely like my mother. The ideal family, mother, father, child - is this what she desired? And then my own arrival, a baby far less pretty than my sister, sometimes ailing and difficult. Did Miriam realise for the first time, with this second child, that domestic life might become a trap?

My father, crumpled as always, holding me to his shoulder, an informal snapshot, neither of us looking towards the camera.

After a time, our parents' presence in the photographs diminishes. My sister and myself, heroic toddlers taking our first brave steps, small legs outstretched as if to walk the plank, no less adventurous than any blindfold pirate. Then as children becoming recognisable, becoming gradually ourselves, coming forward to meet the backward process of memory. Lucy and myself again, cat-slim and puppy-fat, in a further procession of school uniforms – strange the things that do not change. Old-fashioned bucket and spade holidays, family cricket on the sands, taking shelter from the wind beneath rocks, wild hair blown over brave smiles.

Was she happy enough at last, as housewife and mother? Or did she dislike the buckets and spades, the upheavals of family life, the glooms of teenagers? But as with so many women of that time, she had no choice, only duty, the only choice to do it willingly, or not. I had always admired in her the capacity to seem content with very little.

When Lucy and I left home at last, she returned to work for a few years. My father told me once that sometimes she would sing about the house again, as she had done in the early years of their marriage. She had a sweet voice, but I hardly heard it during the time that we were growing up. She did not listen much to music; it seemed to give her no especial pleasure.

Another album: relatives, visitors. My father's mother, Charlotte, so like him, but almost blind now in this picture. She had stayed with us often. She had been suddenly and early widowed, left with four children. And here is a very old snapshot, indefinably foreign, out of place surely amongst these domestic ones - my father's family, also a large one, of European origin, artists, musicians, and academics, their lives terribly shaken by the Second World War. They had many Jewish friends. A cousin of my father's, Leon: at the start of the war, a refugee from central Europe, Vienna I believe – like many artists and musicians, he had found that his work became impossible then - he stayed with my newly-married parents for a year before leaving for the wider horizons of the USA. I was not born then, my sister was still a baby. Sometimes, as I grew older, I wondered about those times, and why my parents had spoken to me so little about them. My father sometimes recalled the foreign phrases that Leon had used; my mother, for whom it must have been a harder thing entirely, said nothing. With her simple background, how could she relate to this strange, exotic figure with his tragic history, suddenly become a part of her own small family, disturbing its symmetry?

I wondered for the first time now where Leon might be, and I hoped that he might have a family of his own.

In all those pictures of my father's relatives, I noticed for the first time their strong likeness - some families are like, some not at all. In my own, I realised, we were all different in our appearance, as if we were hardly related. I was quite unlike my mother, though I resembled my father in many ways, my sister not at all.

I wondered if resemblance, or its opposite, affects the way that families connect with one another; does likeness bring closer ties?

My father's retirement from the university, a group of his colleagues at their farewell dinner. He looked dry and awkward, as ever. He died a few months after that occasion - he must have been ill even then. I wondered again about what might have held my parents together during all the years. Since my own marriage had broken apart, I thought often about this. An attraction of opposites perhaps, as individuals, and as families? Was their marriage already under strain when I was born? Was her chill towards me the result of the difficulties she felt then? Was her sense of duty, always so strong, all that held her marriage and her family together at that time?

As I looked through all the pictures of the past, I realised how little I knew of my parents' lives, of the lives they had lived before I was born.

The last few photographs now, my mother as an old lady, on her own, more beautiful than ever, the fine lines of her bones more marked in age. Her cloudy white hair emphasised the deep intensity of her eyes, not faded nor lessened, though one was now unseeing, as dark within as its outward appearance. The picture recalled somehow that first one of her as a baby, though now she is at the furthest end of her life. She seems as calm, facing her last journey, as determined, as when she set out all those years ago, to her first place of work. She looks at the camera again; serene, fulfilled.

I leant back and closed my eyes for a moment, and I wondered what could be the source of this serenity. Was it only the knowledge of duty done? I had never considered this question, one thinks of these things only when it is too late.

Our parents are, for most of our lives, too close, so that we cannot see them clearly.

At the very bottom of the cupboard, beneath all the letters and albums, I found a small folder, differently shaped, flat. Some papers wrapped in tissue, fragile like aged skin. Writing in my mother's hand, some in a hand I did not know. Very tired now, but feeling that I must continue the task until the end, I undid the ribbon and looked at what was within.

I drew out old sheets of music, yellowing and crumbled at the edges, the fretted coastline of a strange country; inlets, bays, sharp creeks. The notes, hand-written, black and firm, very clear still. A song: the text written beneath it, a piano accompaniment. I looked at the words. It was a love song; at the top, a dedication, a woman's name simply - my mother's.

Then the composer's name.

Below that, another song, a gentle lullaby, a dedication at the top: "To An Unknown Child". I read the music, it was full of longing and love, written, strangely, for a man's voice alone, without accompaniment. There was something of Central or Eastern Europe in the angles of its melody. The composer's name.

It was three in the morning. I opened the old family piano - perhaps he had played it too. It was out of tune now, the pedal groaning. I lit candles upon it, and I played the songs that my father had written, songs to the woman he loved and could not marry, and to his child, whom he could never know nor see.

And I thought of the years he had had in the beautiful city which he had loved and had to leave.

I wondered if he had written more music after he left England. I thought of his years in America, and I hoped that they had at last been good years.

From: Allam, Charlton and Phillips
Solicitors and Notaries

Dear Mrs David,
I should like to send my most sincere condolences on your recent bereavement. I have been pleased to advise your late mother, Mrs Miriam Hecht, over the last fifteen years, and I hope you will not feel it inappropriate if I say that I have come to feel in some measure, over these years, that I have become a friend not only to her, but also to her family. Please understand that I will be happy to advise you in any way I can, in the future, should you wish to contact me.

Your mother asked me to write to you on the event of her death, certain conditions also obtaining. She wished you to learn of the details that follow from myself and no-one else, and she asked me to state that apart from one individual, whose identity will become clear to you as you read this, no other person knows anything concerning the matters referred to in this letter.

I am aware that some of what follows may come as a shock to you. I repeat that should you wish to consult with me on any matter during the next few months, I will be only too happy to help in any way I can.

The next section of the letter told me something of the events surrounding Leon's arrival in this country, which I already knew. Then it continued:

Leon was troubled and unhappy, having left behind many family members and friends in a difficult and dangerous situation. Robert was for much of this time engaged with his professional concerns, and later, often abroad on wartime intelligence duties; your mother was of course at home with a young baby. During those months, Leon and your mother became deeply attached. In due course a baby was born of their relationship, that baby being yourself, as you may already have guessed.

Your mother and Leon Hecht knew that there was no possibility of pursuing their relationship without hurt to your father and sister. Your mother felt always that her first duty was to her husband and older child. In due course, Leon left England to start a new life in America, where I understand he pursued a successful career as a musician. However, your mother and Leon kept in some communication over the years, their objective in this matter being to discuss and decide upon any matters to do with your own welfare. I understand that although Leon did subsequently marry, the marriage was not blessed with other children, and over the years he maintained an understandable interest in your own progress. It was he who supported and paid for your years of study abroad, which your mother felt, owing to Robert's illness, they could not finance at that time.

Leon Hecht died very suddenly, a few months ago, aged about 80, I understand, an event which I believe may have hastened your mother's final illness.

Your parents had agreed that when Leon died, but not until then, you should be told the identity of your true father, if by that time Robert Hecht was also deceased.

Your parents also agreed that Leon's estate should be left to you entirely, as he has no remaining family now, nor heirs, his own wife having died some five years ago. I enclose all the documentation concerning this matter.

Your mother also requested me to ensure that all letters, jewellery and gifts given to her by Leon during the course of their relationship, which she placed recently in my keeping, should also be passed to yourself, as and when the necessary stages of probate have been completed. All correspondence between Miriam and Leon Hecht was sent through my office. Copies of some of these letters are available should you wish to consult them.

I also enclose separately a letter from your mother addressed directly to you, which she asked me to forward to you at the appropriate time.

With kind regards.
Yours faithfully

Frederick Allam

And after a moment I opened the letter that my mother had written to me. The form of the music cannot become clear until the last notes have been heard.

BEER AND BOMBS

Ian Douglas

As the tiny Lao Aviation plane dropped hastily from the sky, I wondered why on Earth I had risked flying to Phonsavan. The answer was, of course, the famous 'Plain of Jars'. These ancient stone vessels lay scattered throughout this far-flung Lao province, and according to the travel books, were fast becoming a tourist magnet. I was looking forward to some hardcore sightseeing.

But Phonsavan has more sinister mysteries lying out on its mountains than Neolithic jars. Acres of grassland appeared below, pockmarked with craters like a lunar landscape, the tragic scars of the Vietnam War. These craters, as I was to learn, were the least of our problems.

From the tiny, dusty airport, I hopped on a tuk-tuk into Phonsavan, an ugly concrete town surrounded by bleak barren slopes – an unearthly vista. I felt as if I were day-tripping to Mars. This barren landscape, I figured, had probably come courtesy of the Americans' use of Agent Orange in Laos.

Alongside the Vietnam War the United States waged what is often known as the 'Secret War'. The Pentagon generals were well aware that the Viet Cong ferried supplies and weapons across Lao into Vietnam. Therefore, they felt justified in bombing Lao in a campaign that was kept away from the world's attention. This included the use of the deadly toxin Agent Orange, dropped by aerial bombardment, which poisoned all foliage and vegetation. In doing so it stripped the communist rebels of the cover they needed for their guerrilla tactics. It also contaminated the soil for years to come, and may be responsible for the many birth defects now seen in the former French colonies of Indo-china. God bless America.

Booked into a cabin at a reasonably clean home-stay I set out to explore the humble streets. Drifting into a cheap café for lunch, I chanced upon a middle-aged Brit whom we'll call Basil. He was a handsome older fellow with an air of action about him. Nevertheless poor Basil was desperate for conversation and fell upon me, inviting me to join his table. Still weary from a week full of shenanigans in Vientiane I was not overly pleased. By now I had travelled all over the world alone and had made peace with the demon of loneliness. I had become a self-sufficient loner who did not need the company of other westerners to legitimate his existence. However Basil did and it would have been unspeakably churlish to decline. Over a couple of Beer Laos and a bowl of steamy noodles he told me his story.

Basil was a bomb disposal expert. Oh yes, the stuff of heroes! Following a distinguished career with the British Army, he had taken early retirement. Eager to make the world a better place, he volunteered for the UN bomb disposal project, and they flew him straight to Phonsavan. Basil, who had never been to Asia, now found himself in one of the most inaccessible slices of the continent. Bleak mountains ringed him in. As there were no safe roads the only way out or in was by plane. There were no other ex-pats or native speakers of English to befriend. Basil was suffering massive culture shock, and I did my best to empathise.

"Some days I turn up for work and my trainees have forgotten to fill the Jeep with petrol! They tell me to take the day off! How can they forget something as crucial as petrol?" he wailed.

Unlike Basil I had already lived in the tropics for some time. So I was familiar with the culture of 'take it easy', (or *baw pen yan* as the Laos say.). Never do today what you can put off till tomorrow. Which is not as odd it sounds in the heat and humidity of South East Asia!

But it was a lot more serious than that. Basil told me there were enough unexploded bombs left over from the Secret War in this province to keep him busy for another five hundred years; pineapples, daisy-cutters, bomblets, the whole deadly assortment. Only the day before, he'd found two live missiles underneath a busy children's classroom. Later in my tour I would see Hmong habitations that were built from discharged shell casings.

The focus of Basil's job was to train up local lads to be defusers themselves. They were brave, good-hearted souls, but so gung-ho to get stuck in he feared for their lives.

Suddenly we were interrupted. A man I recognized from the plane strolled in looking for Basil.

"He's very high up in the government," my newfound friend whispered in my ear. That would explain the leather jacket, a pricey item in a country that can't afford roads. Basil, clearly a man of action, was none too happy to see the politician. He invited me to dine with them that evening, to help smooth over any embarrassing silences. Although I was not keen myself to get drawn in, it seemed discourteous to turn down his request.

The dusk reunited the three of us in a cheap noodle shop. Overhead the blackened mountains were rapidly swallowing up the sun in an orgy of red and orange. Phonsavan, with its elevation above sea level, was less hot than you'd expect and a chill began to creep down from the mountains. Weary, weather-beaten peasants trudged by, returning home from whatever it was they did all day. Twilight in the tropics always has that magical quality, a dark seduction, where it is easy to believe in ghosts. Silently I slurped up my pork ball noodles, enjoying that seduction, while Basil and the bureaucrat exchanged manly, beery banter.

As it happens, Phonsavan only gets four hours of electricity a day, from six pm till ten. Sure enough, come the hour, the light bulbs dimmed and died, as lanterns lit up throughout the town. No longer able to see their beer, Basil and his superior decided to shoot off to a second venue and Basil pleaded with me to go along as the icebreaker.

So there I was, sat in the Unexploded Bomb Land Rover, speeding out into the dark deserted moors. All around was nothing but black fields and bombs. On we drove, up and down, over hills and through vales. Then abruptly...there it was!

Magically, from nowhere, before my astonished eyes appeared...a disco, ablaze with fairy lights. Had I stumbled into Never-Never Land? A few miles away the country folk of Phonsavan were climbing into their hard paupers' beds with nothing to light the way but candles. Was the town's electric supply switched off so that government officials, drug-runners and other nogoodniks could boogie?

The interior was a Spartan, beer-sodden hall. A few depressed-looking waitresses half-heartedly danced the *lam yai*. Dangerous-looking individuals swigged beer, guns poking from their jackets. Our politician offered me my choice of waitress, but I politely declined. I kept my mouth shut and my eyes firmly on my beer. This joint had all the charm of a Wild West saloon on the brink of a shootout. Not to mention the sea of bombs outside. Walk fifty paces in any direction and... BOOM!

I must confess to a blend of curiosity and fear. The former because this was such an unlikely place for little old western me to find myself. We were a very, very, very long way off the tourist trail. The latter due to ticking time bomb of tension I sensed in the air. After all, alcohol and guns really don't mix.

Luckily, both Basil and I kept our heads down and this seemed to avoid trouble.

The government officer was obviously hoping for a wild night of beer and girls, and I guess I must have been a disappointment to him. He spoke scant English, but my overall impression was not one of a man of integrity. Eventually we made our excuses and left, leaving the man from the ministry happily ogling the dancing girls. So there you are. Even in the mountains of Laos there's always somewhere to get drunk and laid, if you know the right people.

As we motored back to Phonsavan's version of civilisation, I pondered my companion. It's true to say that left-wing liberals like me find it difficult to bond with macho army types like Basil. On the other hand, his sacrifice of time and safety to the people of Laos deserved nothing but awe and admiration. I had come to respect him, despite the problems he was clearly finding in adjusting to local customs. Usually I can't stand westerners who come out to Asia and whinge. As a famous Catholic missionary in Bangkok once told me: shut up or ship out. Perhaps my encounter with Basil taught me not to expect others to live up to my standards.

And what did Basil think of me? Although we will never know, I suspect he mistook my reserve and lack of British chumminess for snobbery. Oh those Brits! In their own homeland they would die rather than speak to a stranger. But drop them in foreign climes and they are all over one another like birds of a feather. My view is why bother travelling at all if you are going to hang out with fellow Brits? I always make a point of hanging out with the locals. Nothing personal, Basil!

Basil was a definitive action man, a hero dedicated to beer and bombs. I wondered which of the two gave him the most satisfaction out here in this lonely outpost of humanity. Sadly, only the bombs will never run out.

Some time after midnight, Basil dropped me outside my slumbering guesthouse. Above us the stars, unsullied by city lights, shone in great fuzzy sparkles of silver. Basil roared off, no doubt mindful of the coming day, risking life and limb yet again. He left me choking on his dust.

TRANSIT

Diana Peasey

I have lived a life in transit. A history of comings and goings. A pattern of friendships, break-ups, packing, storing, and unpacking. Of boxes, crates and suitcases, living in many places over the years. Tents, hotels, boarding school, halls of residence and houses, of course. Some of them though, I could never call my home.

They were part of that temporary phase of being. Having arrived from somewhere and yet not there. Suspended in time, waiting for departure. Twice, I have been holed up in a hostel. Decisions in making, transforming our lives. Hoping for a plane that would take me away from a colonial crisis or a car journey to a new future. The circumstances were beyond my control.

The first time followed the shooting of two Servicemen's wives on the island of Cyprus. An emergency was declared putting the British on a twenty-four-hour standby for evacuation. That night, decisions were being made in our villa over which possessions should be put into travelling trunks and packing cases. We waited for the order which would confirm our departure. The boxes packed, the suitcases locked, water supply turned off.

We sat on the verandah, a family in transit. Waiting to be transferred to the hostel in a capital, beset with violence. Eventually, a military policeman showed up, the standby had been stood down. The water supply was switched back on, but the crates and suitcases remained ready for exit. Two weeks later, we were taken under escort to Nicosia, put up in a hotel. Our departure was expected to be the next day, no one ventured onto the streets where so many soldiers had been killed. We stayed put, hoping that time would pass quickly. After all, it was only a short journey away from the airport and then a flight back to the UK. However, the path of transition is never smooth. All military planes in Cyprus had been diverted to a place where there was an even greater flap. Jordan had erupted, hostilities had evoked an emergency plan and it became the latest country where the Brits were pulling out. The troops had to be evacuated so our flight from Cyprus was cancelled. We had to wait for the situation to calm down for the planes to become available. There was also another shooting on the streets of Nicosia along 'Sniper Alley', as it was called. A curfew imposed. Our family would have to get used to life in a hotel room.

Transit

For me it was just one big adventure. That's how I coped with the difficulties, I was just eight. At Salamis Road, in Famagusta I loved scrambling over fences to tell people a curfew was about to begin, or wandering into the orange groves to find the terrorists. I would shout with joy when the planes flew over dropping propaganda leaflets urging their leader General Grivas to give himself up. For me the leaflets would provide the material to make my homemade kites.

There was nothing we could do about the long wait that October in Nicosia. The problem with being in transit is you can't go back. Only forwards when you have the means to do so. Those means were the planes in Jordan. Eventually, they arrived. We embarked on a flight home to a dark, foggy London where we would stay in a cold, terraced house belonging to my grandfather.

Years later, my family spent more than a few weeks in a hostel in Southsea, near Portsmouth. It was supposed to be the start of a new beginning. My father was leaving the Army. We had arrived there via a circuitous route from Germany where home had been a place called Wetter, near Dortmund. My father decided to take us on a camping trip across Europe. By now there were three children. We made our way through Holland, Belgium, Luxembourg and France. He viewed it as an opportunity to see some of the sights, informative and educational for us. We took in the trenches of the First World War and the military cemeteries of the Second. We walked along the canals in Amsterdam, and drove around the old motor racetrack at Zandvoort. We paid a visit to Radio Luxembourg which I had listened to illicitly underneath the bedcovers at boarding school until my radio was confiscated. We walked around the magnificent cathedral at Amiens and bought chocolates in Brussels.

Now this family of inveterate travellers were lodgers in a Victorian hotel. To us, it was the army transit hostel and another period of waiting to go elsewhere. The architecture was typical of its generation and big enough to cope with the wandering souls of its inmates. Now sixteen, I had a room to myself although I often had the company of my brother and sister, who were much younger than me. They loved my music. I played my records, over and over again. 'Little Red Rooster', by the Rolling Stones and 'She Loves You' by the Beatles. They didn't seem to understand why I seemed so irritable. Once again, I had been uprooted. Away from my friends, away from a school I liked, away from my blossoming romance with two boys, one German and one English.

One night, I was traumatised by an incident at the hostel. I was awoken by a loud bang of a door down the corridor. And then a woman's cry.

"Please no, no."

I listened to the voice. It wasn't my mother's. The crying developed into screams, and shouts.

"Open your legs, you stupid woman," said the man.

The woman's struggle, her resistance to the drunken ardour of her husband was clear.

"No, no, no, no!" she cried out.

Blows to her body made her submit. The silent hotel heard the whimpers in harmony with the grunts. The snoring which followed the satisfaction of one and the distress of the other. The woman had been raped and I had been psychologically violated.

Next morning, the battered woman came down to breakfast. Her bruised face confirmed the events the night before. She was red-eyed and carried a hanky to dab the tears on her cheeks. She maintained the decorum expected of a military wife. She scooped up her cornflakes and asked for a pot of tea. One of the wives on another table went up to her and asked her if she was all right. The woman nodded. Glances passed from table to table from one wife to another. The husband of one woman told her,

"Keep out of it. It's domestic."

The wife nodded. We sat at another table and my mother urged us to eat our cornflakes.

It's odd how in a life of transit, I had forgotten about the incident until recently. Submerged in a fog of memories of different homes in different countries, the more I thought about what happened that night, the more I began to understand how it had affected me. For a few years after the rape, I would shudder when a man wanted to hold me. I would block any advances until I overcame my fears.

SELECTIVE LIVING

Fay Watkins

Emma disentangled herself from her bulky red coat. She twisted the curl of dark brown hair that tickled her cheek, and pushed it behind her ear.
"Can I get you a drink? Tea or coffee?"
"No, I'm fine." Emma sat in one of two comfy chairs that Paul Mayes had pointed out. She let her deep brown eyes move around the room like a butterfly, touching details; his desk and swivel chair, the overflowing bookcase, a dried out spider plant in the corner. She rubbed her chapped lips together, there would only be remnants of pink lipstick.
"How are you feeling about being here, Emma?"
"Fine, it's not like I haven't said it all before, is it?" There'd been so many interviews she'd started to feel it wasn't her speaking. She heard the words but they lacked emotion, like someone had turned off the electricity to the television but it still worked.
"No, I know it can't be easy for you but I want you to feel comfortable. If there's anything you need, let me know. If you want to take a break at any point just say, we've got plenty of time...okay?"
She nodded.
"Shall we start with how you and Steve met?"
She wanted to smile, to give the impression of being a good person. Her lips and cheeks lifted but she knew her eyes were cold from the way people looked at her. She'd noticed the blankness reflected in them. She wanted Paul to see the warmth she used to radiate, not the ice-cold pillar lodged in her gut.
"At work. He was new, he asked me out to see a film. It went from there really. We started seeing each other regularly. He was very attentive, always popping in for a chat. I suppose you know the rest."
"I'm just going to note a few things as we talk." He said. She'd become used to looking at the tops of heads and speedy hands putting the black vapours of her life into print. "What happened after you'd been seeing each other for a while?"
"After about four months, we decided to move into together. We couldn't bear to be apart. Right from the beginning he said he loved me. He'd phone me all the time, just to say it. I remember feeling so lucky."
"What was living together like?"

"Everything changed. He became someone else." This was the part she couldn't stop beating herself up about. She couldn't get it clear in her head like a thread she kept pulling and twisting rather than cutting off. Why didn't she leave as soon as she knew the sort of man he was?

"How did he change, Emma?"

"He got really jealous about me seeing friends after work. So he'd come along, which was okay, but he took a dislike to Pete, one of the blokes from the office. He said that he fancied me and I was encouraging him. He wouldn't let it go, he wanted me to look for another job. He said it was too upsetting for him knowing I was with Pete all day."

"And did you find another job?"

"Yeah, eventually, I didn't really want to leave but I wanted him to be happy. But it wasn't long before he didn't want me to go out with friends at all. Not that I went very often, maybe once a month. He said it wasn't me he was worried about, it was other blokes. He knew what they were like. In the end it got so I could only go out with him."

"How did that make you feel?"

"I was flattered to start with; he said it was because he cared about me, was protecting me. No one had ever wanted to do that before."

"What about the violence, when did that start?"

"Not long after we were together really, a few months or so. I'd had a crap day at work, everything went wrong; I'd overcooked the pasta and was rushing because I knew he'd be back soon. I'd not hoovered, and he always got really annoyed if it wasn't done every day. I was irritated, banging pots around. He came in saw the state of everything and we argued. He got so angry he thumped me in the stomach." Emma faltered. The shock was the thing she remembered the most. He'd grabbed her neck and pushed her face into the hot and sticky pasta. He'd lifted and pushed, ramming and grinding his words with her face into the mush.

"He shouted, pull yourself together, you stupid fuckin' cow. Look at the state of this house. All the things I do for you and this is how you repay me. You're useless." He'd readjusted his hold, gripping hard at the back of her neck and threw her against the kitchen wall. She remembered her jaw hitting the wall and the feel of the plaster.

Emma recalled this first time as easily as she recalled the other firsts. The time they'd kissed, danced and made love. Later when he'd raped her, the time he'd locked her in the house, the first time he'd threatened to kill her.

"How often was he violent?"

Selective Living

"I don't know, I didn't count, I didn't realise I was going to have to remember it all, I didn't want to remember." Emma tried to control her anger. Did these people think she should have kept a diary so later she could remember every detail?

"I'm sorry, I know this is difficult. Was it regularly, once a week, once a month?"

"Maybe once a month. I tried to make sure everything was the way he liked it. There were always the times though when he was looking for a fight and nothing I did made any difference."

"Can you tell me about that night, Emma? What happened?"

"We argued. We were supposed to be going out to Sue and Dale's house for dinner."

"What was it about?"

"He told me I looked a state. I could tell he was angry when he came in from work. 'D'you know what you look like?' he said, 'Have you looked in the mirror? You look a fuckin' state."

"What did you do?"

"I said I'd change if it would make him happy. He said it was too late and I'd ruined the evening. He said he could have any woman he wanted and he was lumbered with me."

"How did you feel?"

"I didn't want us to be late. I felt nervous about explaining to Sue and Dale. Partly I thought he was right, I could have made more of an effort..." Emma's voice trailed off.

"What happened next?"

"I started to go upstairs, to get changed and he grabbed my hair. He kept thumping me in the chest and stomach. After, he told me to ring and cancel. He said there was no way he was going out with me. I rang Sue, told her I wasn't feeling well. He overheard me and wanted to know why she was bothered about me, it was him she should be asking about. He didn't like anyone showing any interest in me, man or woman. I suppose he was afraid I'd tell someone."

"Did you ever tell anyone?"

"No. Sue did ask me and I was off work with cracked ribs after that time. But I told her he'd never do anything to hurt me. I told her I'd fallen down the stairs. I was scared of not convincing her."

"Why was she suspicious?"

"She didn't like the way he spoke to me sometimes. He could be the perfect gentleman, but there were times he let the mask slip. He was always careful not to cause too much damage after that first time though."

"What happened after you'd made the phone call?"

"He dragged me upstairs to our bedroom, saying he was going to teach me a lesson. He made me take off my clothes." Emma looked at the box of tissues on the white scratched surface of the table between her and Paul. She remembered the promise to herself earlier, not to cry.

"Can you go on? Do you need a break?"

"No – I'm sorry, I'll be okay in a minute."

"What happened?"

"He raped me..." Emma leant her elbows on her knees and held her head in her hands. How many more times would she have to talk about this before it stopped hurting? She struggled not to be wrenched back to that room. Something more than him ramming himself into her had happened that day. She couldn't put it in words. It was like he'd obscured every loving moment by violating her with his poison.

"Had he sexually assaulted you before?"

"Yes."

"What happened after?"

"He told me to get dressed and get his tea, said he was starving. I went downstairs and took the carving knife out of the kitchen drawer."

"What were you thinking at the time?"

"Nothing... I don't remember. I shouted him saying it was ready. He was moaning that it had better be good. I hid the knife under the newspaper on the worktop. He came in and got angry because he couldn't see anything cooking. I took the knife from under the newspaper and stabbed him in the chest."

"Emma, why did you call the emergency services?"

"I didn't want him to die. I just wanted him to stop."

"What happened when the Police arrived?"

"They had to force the door." Emma could remember phoning and telling the woman on the emergency services line that she'd stabbed Steve, but she couldn't remember hearing the Police thumping on the door. "I remember the face of one of the policemen. He looked so young. He took the knife from my hand, there was blood stuck to the blade, and the handle was sticky. My hand felt tight, I remember trying to stretch out my fingers. You don't normally see that much blood do you? I never realised there'd be so much blood."

"Emma, in the police reports it describes you having extensive bruising and cigarette burns to your body and arms." She tugged at the cuffs of her sleeves, as if exposed. "When did you sustain these?"

"A couple of days before. He beat me because I was late back from work, the battery on my mobile was flat. He kept saying I was seeing someone else."

"And the cigarette burns?"
"He said that no man would want me if I was scarred."
"Did you ever try to leave, Emma?"
"No. I couldn't. He said he'd kill me. It's funny; I can talk to anyone about it now. You, the police, a stranger in Asda, I don't even know you. And I never told a living soul for years, not one. Yet now it's all I talk about, it's all anyone wants to know about me."
"How do you feel about the pregnancy?"
"How would you feel?" She was tiring of it all, the questions.
"Have you thought about the future?"
"Yes, when I'm not talking about the past." She tried to smile but it didn't work. Nothing worked. She couldn't feel what she needed to, to make the smile genuine. "The papers have approached me for my story, and there's a possibility of a book. I'm considering it. I'll need the money whatever happens."
"I'm not surprised by the media attention you've had, Steve was an unlikely abuser, and people thought they knew him, his death has created a lot of attention."
"My solicitor thinks there's a chance I could get acquitted, there's a defence category, Battered Woman Syndrome. If I'm found guilty then hopefully I'll get to keep the baby with me in a prison with a special unit, at least for a while anyway. That's why I'm here isn't it?"
"Yes, that's right. My assessment report will go to your solicitor and barrister and if they think it will help I can speak on your behalf in court."
"Do you think it will help? I mean do you think I have a chance?" Emma could feel the tears she'd held back filling her eyes.
"I think you have a slim chance of being acquitted and starting your life over Emma. Steve was perceived by the public as being a loveable, friendly, caring man, convincing them that he was a monster and that your only way out of the relationship was murder won't be easy though. Maybe the best you can hope for is manslaughter and a judge who is sympathetic."

HOW DID THAT GET THERE?

Ronan Fitzsimons

The angle-poise lamp cast its beam down onto Arthur's bench, cutting through the darkness of the workshop. Carefully, with the skill acquired over nearly forty years as a practitioner, he held a shiny white plimsoll up to the light, gauged what needed to be done, and set about his task. Sitting on a stool behind him, Steph, his sixteen-year-old apprentice, looked earnestly over his shoulder, drinking in the craft performed by the hands of her master. Outside, under a clear, sharp Batley night, young Tom pulled up on the module, clambered off and stood smoking nearby, blowing rings up into the sky and awaiting the next consignment.

Most analyses of late-twenty-first-century history overlook the important decision taken by the Liberal Democrat government to privatise the distribution of used plimsolls along the central reservations of Britain's motorways and dual carriageways. Scant mention is afforded to the groundwork done by the Labour predecessors, who oversaw the infrastructure changes necessary to convert motorway crash barriers into a monorail system to facilitate accurate and safe dissemination. Up to 2053, dispersal of trainers had relied partly on the slovenly crew of government employees and their occasional burst of daredevil endeavour, and partly on the goodwill of nocturnal motorway cone-planters, always willing to take a bung and give the regular lads a night off. But now, as a result of the Lib Dems' foresight, it was all very different.

It was a difference Arthur pondered as he put his glasses on again and inspected his handiwork. With the laces removed, this particular specimen had been virginal, so the distressing he had to perform was pleasingly uniform. The tools of his trade made this second nature to him: sanders, buffers, mudpack applicators, sole scuffers and crackers, stitching unpickers, eyelet removers and instep mis-shapers. He spun around on his stool and showed the example to Steph, looking at her over the top of his glasses.

"You see how I've altered the shape of the instep?" he told her. "It's all very well creating a uniform dirtiness – any chump can do that – but it's your detail, your unpicking of the seams, your twisting of the sole, that's what separates your craftsman from your amateur."

Steph nodded keenly and took the plimsoll from Arthur to scrutinise it. He'd done a marvellous job, as ever. There was something uncanny about the consistency with which Arthur could bang out crate after crate of impeccably deformed, highway-ready sports shoes. More than that, she was convinced there was something special about him. He wasn't just a craftsman. Something else was eating away at her, but she couldn't put her finger on exactly what. She turned the shoe over and marvelled at what, ten minutes previously, had been a pristine item of footwear, freshly lifted from a Famous Army and Navy Store in Huddersfield. Now it was scuffed almost beyond recognition, a pallid grey, lacking in shape and utterly useless for all purposes bar one. This was what she liked most about this modern apprenticeship: seeing the fruits of her mentor's craft. The stuff she learned at college on day release was all well and good, but this was the real thing, the peak of what the profession she was living and breathing could produce. She kissed the plimsoll, leaving a pink smear on its flank, and handed it back to Arthur, nodding and smiling in hushed reverence.

Arthur tossed this last of the shoes into a large metal crate alongside his bench, and yawned noisily, stretching his arms and back after hours of being hunched over his work.

"I'll leave you to lock up, then, lass, eh?" he said to Steph. "Just make sure 'is nibs gets this last delivery off to Pontefract by midnight, otherwise we'll not get the last connection for the A1."

"Sure," replied Steph. "Leave it with me, Mr Schofield. See you tomorrow morning."

"Night, lass," said Arthur with a smile. Then he looked at the floor for a few seconds, coughed slightly and turned his gaze to his protégée. "I reckon you're ready to be trusted on the shoes yourself. Shall we start you off tomorrow, lass? It'd give me a bit of a rest. I'm a weary old man now."

With that, he walked out of the workshop, stretched again, and looked up to where the company's green, blue and indigo communication beams were drifting listlessly by, no specific task to occupy them at present. He took a deep breath, closed his eyes and frowned for a long while, then nodded ferociously in the direction of the beams. The green beam twitched into life, and within nanoseconds two other parts of the north of England had been alerted to Arthur's message. The wheels were in motion.

As she helped Tom clip the crate of trainers to the module outside, Steph could barely conceal her pride at rising so sharply in her guru's estimations.

"Can't you see," she said to the HQ logistics controller, "this could be my big breakthrough. If he's entrusting me with the preparation of the shoes, it might mean he'll hand over the whole business to me eventually. He can't be far off retirement, can he?"

"No, you could be right," Tom responded with a warm smile. He took her by the hand. "Look, I'd better get this lot over to Pontefract. Fancy a ride?"

Steph spotted his smirk and smacked him playfully around the chops. She turned round, checked the workshop door was locked, pocketed the keys and jumped nimbly aboard the module alongside Tom.

Arthur sat in his favourite armchair at home, cradling a hefty whisky. Despite the successes of the day – finishing the Pontefract order on time, and the undoubted progress being made by young Stephanie – his mood was dark and troubled. The bloody authorities were meddling in his affairs once again. The government's magnanimous policies and election of Arthur's firm, Highway Plimsoll Allocation Ltd, as sole footwear suppliers to the UK's roads were all fine and dandy, but the minister's insistence on left-foot trainers a couple of years later had proved a nightmare. All the shoe shops and other distribution streams via which Arthur bought, begged or pilfered his stock displayed only right-foot items, and this had been the case for as long as he or any of his associates could remember. Then the buggers insisted on left.

So he'd set about revising his sourcing system, eschewing all the traditional shoe shops across West Yorkshire and moving into shadier areas of warehousing scams and the ambushing of Clark's delivery lorries. It cost him a lot of favours and a fair chunk of his profits initially, but he'd finally landed the right number and consistency of deals to see him through.

Now this latest caper. How the hell was he expected to solve this one? Arthur reached for the bottle of whisky and topped up his glass. Nursing his tipple, he sat rheumy-eyed and stony-faced, glaring at the wall opposite and trying to figure out how to out-manoeuvre the might of Brussels.

Under a deep blue canopy of plush velvet sky, Tom and Steph hurtled smoothly eastwards towards Pontefract. Time was on their side: it was not yet eleven thirty, so Tom overrode the auto-velocitator and eased back on their speed. Steph stroked his leg absent-mindedly, her thoughts focused on days ahead.

"Tom," she began, her voice sounding calm and faintly dreamy, "once we've dropped the stuff off, do you fancy going for a cruise round somewhere? We could, you know... talk."

"Sure," said Tom, beaming at her. "We've put in enough hours for the company today."

A few minutes later they glided to a halt at the Pontefract modular interchange, where the regional distribution co-ordinator greeted them with a nervous smile.

"What's up?" joked Tom. "Has the cat pissed in your methane tank again?"

"Worse than that," replied the man solemnly. "The A1 lads have called a strike, and I can't get the buggers to budge. I even offered to pay them a bonus out of my own pocket, but they were having none of it. Matter of principle, they said. Bollocks, I say. A euro in your pocket is a euro extra to spend. Sod the bloody principles."

"So what happens with the Newcastle run tonight, then?" enquired Tom, unhooking the crate from the module and hefting it onto the platform.

The regional co-ordinator nibbled his stylus and pretended to be immersed in something on the screen of his wrist-top.

"Oh, you've got to be kidding," protested Tom. "We're both done in. I've been on the go since half-six this morning."

"Pretty please," implored the co-ordinator. "I wouldn't ask if I wasn't desperate."

"So your wife told me," quipped Tom, realising that the guy was in dire straits. He looked at Steph, who shrugged in a manner that suggested she was up for it if he was. "Go on, then, just this once. Which module do you want us to take?"

"I've got it all set up here. The auto-footwear-dispenser is set to release a plimsoll every 4.5 miles, which is the maximum allowed, assuming a constant velocity, which I've also set for you. The beauty of this machine is that it even does the alternating deposits for you: west and east carriageways, so that you get a balanced effect. And it ensures that the shoes land the correct way up, at correctly gauged angles so as to give what we call the desired randomly-strewn effect. It's textbook stuff. The lads over on the M6 have to do the alternating thing manually, shifting the chute after every deposit. Poor bastards."

Tom and Steph nodded sagely, clipped their crate into place on the spanking new module and mounted up. Tom fired the motor up, and it purred gently, a relief after the clattering chaos of the regional delivery capsule. With a friendly salute to the co-ordinator, they eased off northwards, sliding effortlessly in the direction of Wetherby and the northeast beyond. As they disappeared from view, the co-ordinator rushed over to his hut, picked up his inter-wave device and quickly dialled up a number in Batley.

Arthur had now finished his whisky, and was re-reading the document he'd had sent over from the ministry.

Westminster, 6 October

Dear Mr Schofield

Further to our recent contact, I can confirm that the EU resolution we discussed has now been approved in principle, and is due to come into force on 1 January next year. As you may imagine, what I have received from Brussels is a weighty tome covering all sorts of distribution industries and services, but the section relating to Highway Plimsoll Allocation Ltd can be summarised as follows:

"…plimsoll distribution on highways in member States is to be revised. Any State wishing to remain part of the Europe-wide scheme must ensure that the agency carrying out the distribution deposits a maximum of one plimsoll every 12 kilometres. To prevent duplication or unseemly cluttering of the highways of our continent, existing deposits must be removed before implementation of this new measure. Failure to adhere to the 12-kilometre separation clause will be punished with a fine of €3,000 per non-conforming interval discovered."

I know you will be disappointed to read this, as it will imply a vast restructuring of your rolling stock, but I hope that, in the spirit of European harmony, you will be able to adapt your business accordingly. Please let me know if I can be of any administrative – though alas, not financial – assistance.

Yours sincerely
Ron Doodler
Department of Logistic Policy

Arthur shook his head sadly. "Bastards," he said. But by now his mind was made up. There was only one thing for it. Then the inter-wave device rang. He picked it up and listened to a voice giving him specific information.

"Good," said Arthur a minute or so later. "We'll go ahead as planned, then. The beams are on stand-by, they just need full activation."

The trip north was going like a dream. Any concerns Tom and Steph might have had about the future now dissipated as the cool wind raced through their hair. As they passed Wetherby, Tom looked back and saw to his delight that the auto-footwear-dispenser was working perfectly, coinciding precisely with the time, distance and carriageway-side indicated on his summary screen. He relaxed, and turned to face Steph.

"I love you," he felt prompted to say. As he reached in to kiss her and their lips touched, they both thought they felt something strange happen, a tickling force of energy which passed straight through them. At the same time, a howling gale raged and began to vacuum up all the previously deposited plimsolls and whisk them away to safe ground away from the highways. Without thinking, Tom reached for the auto-velocitator button and cranked up their speed. It might well have an impact on the accuracy of the footwear feeding process, he thought, but something within him suggested there were more critical concerns at play.

"I love you too," said Steph, raising her voice and gripping her seat all the harder.

They sped on, and Tom noticed on his screen that the release of plimsolls was now happening at intervals of 7.5 miles, reckless by anyone's standards. How the country would manage with such a sparse distribution of used footwear was beyond him, but it was something with which the nation would just have to learn to live. But what worried him more was the module itself. The increased speed and feeding seemed to be taking its toll on the machine's smoothness: the feline grace with which it had begun its journey had now been replaced by a lupine growl, but again, Tom had to banish such anxieties from his mind.

"Can't you slow it down?" complained Steph, a note of wavering panic in her voice. "It's starting to get a bit scary."

Tom thought for a moment.

"There's no way I can reduce our speed. It just doesn't feel right. Sorry. But whatever happens, you know we'll be together," he yelled back. It wasn't vintage Hollywood, but it was the best he could manage under the circumstances.

Faces set, they careered northwards towards their destiny.

Elsewhere in the country, plimsoll distribution specialists were experiencing similar unease. On the M42, one module had surpassed its maximum velocity and was performing a breakneck (but pleasingly arbitrary) shedding of its cargo, also at gaps of 7.5 miles. Two modules were racing round the M25, one in each direction, vomiting trainers with unforeseen alacrity. The drivers had passed each other twice before either had dared raise a set of white knuckles to acknowledge the other. Down past Swindon, the acne-ridden delivery boy had given up trying to rectify the controls of his module, and had assumed an ungainly, arse-first 'brace' posture.

Back in Batley, Arthur staggered back to the workshop. Reaching his bank of controls, he pressed two buttons and set a time-delay on a third, then climbed up to the roof, stood in his special spot and waited, his eyes closed and a tight frown furrowing his brow.

Across the nation, modules were churning out their last plimsoll just as the relevant stretch of motorway or dual carriageway ended, and either crashing or spluttering to a halt. As soon as each driver had escaped from the vehicle, the capsule was bursting into flames, creating a mosaic of vivid colour across vast swathes of Great Britain. Before long, the only module in motion was Tom and Steph's, still tearing up the A1 and rapidly approaching Durham. Steph glanced down into the feeder crate: only two plimsolls remained. The first of these shot down the chute just as they passed the Carville turn-off, leaving only the last shoe, the one Steph had examined so carefully in the workshop with Arthur.

Before they knew what was happening, they took a left-hand bend on the monorail and their speed doubled, whisking them sheer off the track and up into the air. Higher and higher they rose, swirling with the wind, looping over fields and streams and soon encircling the grey towers of Durham Cathedral. Clinging on for dear life, they continued their journey northwards, the capsule now darting headlong towards Gateshead.

"Is this it?" screamed Steph above the noise of the craft.

"Whatever it is, it's you and me," was all Tom could manage before a blinding flash up ahead spelled what could only be their doom. Illuminated bright white, the Angel of the North stood proud, a vast human face at its crux beckoning them in. It was getting nearer and nearer, the light fearsome and the sound deafening. At the point of impact, Arthur's face at the crux smiled benignly and winked as they smashed through his midriff, then there was silence, darkness, utter still.

Opening their eyes, Steph and Tom found themselves sitting on the grass at the foot of the sculpture, the module nowhere to be seen but the feeder crate on the ground next to them. Inside it was a sheet of paper. Steph snatched it up and read it hungrily, discovering to her puzzlement that it was a letter from Arthur. They had done well, he said. Highway Plimsoll Allocation Ltd was no more, he said. But in recompense, he said, here was a cheque for the pair of them, as sole heirs to his carefully squirreled fortune. They lay back and looked up into the sky.

"Thank you, Arthur!" they cried.

With that, the remaining plimsoll fluttered out of the crate, floating away a bit further to the north, settling smack in the middle of the Tyne Bridge. As it touched down, the world resumed its motion, and a business plan began to form in Tom's mind: the random distribution of tatty plastic bags in the hedges of the nation.

BEFORE 1963

John Lucas

That bought-in-the-Med short-sleeved shirt
sported by Reading's poet Ian Fletcher
at an *echt* student party where he alone was staff,
gave, despite his advanced hopes,
no great pulling power.

For poking like limed twigs from an ex-army vest
were arms untainted by Cypriot sun,
and patched, lovat twill trousers could hardly contain
the shirt's mustard and turquoise outbursts.

Yet credit him for trying. 1950s raffish
favoured the eyebrow moustache, fawn
or canary waistcoat, and suede gloves worn to ease
a low-slung roadster up some tree-roofed lane
where lust's expectancies whispered in taffeta shirr.

No whispering while Gene Vincent,
The Big Bopper and Little Richard reeled
in the Dansette's uncertain speed: talk blared,
Ian's his ace "white and hairless as an egg",
loudest of all. So when
the clock stopped as Haley's Comets
ceased to spin, all present were bound to hear
that trumpeted, metrically licentious line,
"Tell, me what are your views on foreplay."

THE HUMAN MIND'S REMARKABLE ABILITY TO REMOVE ITSELF

Adam E. Smith

Something unclear played on the TV, either a consumer affairs programme, or a guide for how to deal with money. Jonathan paid it little attention at first. He was sitting on his saggy bed, his feet propped on an inverted wooden box, with a bowl of microwave noodles in his hand. He twirled the food around his fork and mechanically pushed it into his mouth. Having turned the heater off an hour ago, the bed-sit where he lived was now cold and he wished the food were warmer. Jonathan took another mouthful of food. He was sitting awkwardly on the edge of the bed with his feet propped, and he was at a table in a restaurant in town, flanked by friends and eating steak. The TV flashed an unclear graphic.

The woman on TV looked like she'd been screwed by a high street store. Jonathan couldn't feel anything for her; she exuded arrogance, and looked like she earned enough money. The financial adviser she spoke to wore a tie with a wide knot and a garish pattern. He had short, wet-look hair and a slight tan. Jonathan guessed he was the same age as him, and then he quickly changed the channel, deciding he was paying that one too much interest. Forking another clump of noodles into his mouth and tasting nothing, Jonathan looked over at the little window behind the TV. Through the dusk, he saw the building across the road, the brash glow of a streetlamp and nothing else. The noodles bored him so he put them down and lit a cigarette, using the discarded bowl as an ashtray.

Jonathan stubbed out the cigarette and walked over to the corner of the room where his clothes hung, feeling the cold floor through his socks. He selected the uniform and changed into it, shaking off the discomfort insisted upon by the cotton/acrylic/polyester mix. The uniform still felt scratchy after five years of wearing it nightly. He didn't even look in the grimy little mirror as he passed it, but picked up his cigarettes, lighter, keys and turned off the TV on his way out to work and on his way out to buy a guitar he would learn how to play and impress strangers with. On the street, cold air slapped him.

Jonathan took his usual walk through town. He passed a hen party already out and ready to get drunk. The obvious bride-to-be wore a nurse's outfit and a veil. She wobbled on high heels, and the hue of her hair reminded him of one of his old foster mums. A bright, platinum blonde, he thought, and then pictured himself in the presence of the film star with the same colour hair that he'd seen on a billboard somewhere. He rushed over the damp streets, passed the shuttered shops and beckoning bars. He was walking along the street, and he was in one of those bars sipping a pint. The buildings changed as he walked; he was now in a part of town he felt far from, yet he knew its streets so well. Jonathan recalled being a teenager on these streets, practically living on them. He knew them; but he didn't feel close to them.

Jonathan was ten years old when his parents were sent to prison and he remembered the house of his first foster family as having stained glass in the front door. The door of his place of work had stained glass also, but its trendy design was not as intricate. It was split into two panels: one clear and one red. Yet it always made him picture the boat on the door of that foster family. He pushed open the door and nodded to the man behind the desk, who raised an eyebrow only.

The Human Mind's Remarkable Ability to Remove Itself

Jonathan dumped his jacket, cigarettes, lighter and keys in the staff room off to the right of the lobby and then met the man on the desk.
"Evening," he muttered.
"Hi."
The man closed the crossword book he was working in and stood. He pointed to the TV screen mounted above the desk and said, "Stairwell Two got some crap needs clearing. That's it."
"OK."
The man made a quick visit into the staff room and then left through the front doors, soon to be home with his family. Jonathan sat down at the desk and looked around the big, bland lobby of the apartment building. Minimalist, he'd heard it described as. Like that gallery. His nose wrinkled and he looked at the computer screen, adjusting it slightly to the right to cut out the glare from the ceiling light. He noticed the pen pot was back over on the other side of the desk too. He moved to reposition it but didn't bother; it would only get changed the next day. Jonathan picked out a pencil and tapped its end on the desk. His watch read nine p.m. and he sat staring at the white walls and it read nine a.m. and he was parking a nice car under an office block. Glancing up at the TV screen, he recalled the cleaning job and walked out to complete it, placing the fast food cartons in a black bin liner and in turn, throwing that in the big metal container outside. He sat back down at the desk. A resident with a briefcase swiped his card through a reader on the stained glass door and entered, giving Jonathan a curt and forced smile. Jonathan gave a single nod and watched as the man waited impatiently for the lift to return, the briefcase twitching in his hand. The man, the briefcase, the shiny floor: they all slotted together. Jonathan shifted his weight uneasily in the chair.

Jonathan opened a game of Solitaire on the computer and absentmindedly started to play. He stared at the computer screen and he watched the football match closely, feeling the crowd around him, the cup of tea in his hand. His team had just let a goal in but now the ball was with their star striker. He completed Solitaire twice and then closed the program, looking around the lobby. After an hour and a half the chair became uncomfortable so Jonathan stood and walked around the edges of the room. More residents arrived home; he gave them a nod and they chiefly ignored him. Most saw him daily but spoke little. Occasionally he got called up to their apartment to change a fuse for them, or be informed about a drunkard seen hanging about on the street on their way home. But mostly he sat in the chair and looked at the walls. And he sat in a padded leather desk chair and received calls from people in another part of the company, and had his boss come out of his office to congratulate him on the good work. And then he went home and his girlfriend cooked a meal and they went to the cinema and saw a film about a man trying to find his long-lost son and his girlfriend cried at the end.

A little after midnight, Jonathan went into the staff room to make a cup of tea. To get at the kettle he had to push aside the buckets and mops and sprays the cleaners always dumped on the floor. He waited patiently for the water to boil and looked around at the lockers, the pegs, the two chairs, the mugs. The man he'd relieved earlier had placed everything where they were, Jonathan could tell. The man had worked in the building for years before Jonathan and if something was not done his way, it was done the wrong way. Steam rose from the water as he poured it into the mug. He felt the steam on his face and then he felt it all over his body as he sat in a steam room, like the one in the advert on the TV. Leaving the steam room, he changed into swimming shorts and went for a dip in the heated pool, then met his friends afterwards in the club bar. One of them suggested they go on a city break for their birthday. Jonathan bought the next round of drinks and replied to a text message from his brother. The tea tasted of nothing. He smoked a cigarette, and then another.

By three a.m. the dark outside was uninterrupted by passers-by. Just the occasional taxi and the pervasive streetlamps. Rain had been falling for over an hour and the streets were awash with water. Jonathan pictured it dirtying his trouser legs on his walk back to the bed-sit. He sat at the desk and looked at the TV screen. It was split into four sections, showing different parts of stairwells, and the interior of the lift. He looked really closely at the floor of the lift on the screen and he looked really closely at the paintwork on his new car. It wasn't flashy, but no shed either. He'd made sure to get a lot of extras, but not the ones he didn't need. Metallic paint was a must though, and it looked great on his car. When he upgraded in five years' time, he told himself to get alloy wheels. To match the glossy chrome finish on some interior installations. The air-con would prove handy in summer. He drove through town wearing shades and listening to the radio. The car drove like a dream. Blinking slowly, he shifted his attention from the TV screen to the floor.

At five a.m. a woman came to replace him. She wore a short skirt that showed just enough leg. Her shirt cupped her breasts just right. Jonathan muttered a short hello and than said he had to go. He grabbed his things and walked slowly through town, hearing the rainwater swish at his feet. The rain had stopped but the streets were still soaked. He walked along the beach in Brighton with the chilly sea at his feet. He'd heard it was nice there. Some drivers on the roads were already on their way to work, in uniforms or shirts and ties. They had so much to do that day; all Jonathan had to do was go to the bed-sit where he lived, watch morning TV and then sleep until seven or eight in the evening.

A group of young guys were propped up against a stone wall on a street just off from the town centre. Clearly very drunk, they attempted to sing a tune that Jonathan could not make out. One wore a scarf and a tee-shirt. Another had a diamond earring. They suddenly burst into conversation as Jonathan passed. The one with the scarf slurred something about working in the City when he graduated. Jonathan continued walking to the bed-sit and he continued walking on his way to visit his mother who managed a department store. She usually had time to see him in her lunch hour and they got on so well and Jonathan often went round to her house where she cooked a lovely dinner and they'd reminisce about his childhood and the backyard swing they had. He took a last look at the drunken young men and saw his mother amongst them, and in jail.

The stairs made their usual creak as he ascended them, up to the bed-sit. Turning the key, he pushed the door with the required technique he could never do right and didn't notice the bit of tape stuck to the door. Or the piece of paper that had come unattached from it and drifted down to the floor. Jonathan closed the door behind him, oblivious to the eviction notice on the floor in the hall outside. He was too busy turning on the TV and turning on the lamp in his weekend seaside apartment.

NETS

David Belbin

I saw him at the window again today. For a while I watched him read, or write, I'm not sure. Then he turned and stared at me as if I wasn't there. He sits on his swivel chair, half facing the desk, half facing the window. Now and then he raises his head. Now and then our eyes meet over two back yards. Or would, if I could see his eyes. I am always the one who turns away first. Then I go and sit on my bed, which is to the side of the window, or pull down the red blind. That's another thing. He also has a red blind, the same shade as mine. But he never pulls it down.

Sometimes when I put my make up on in the morning and I look round, he is already there, dressed, at the window of his study. I say it is a study, for it has a desk, and bookshelves, a few plants, and I don't think he sleeps there. Does he go out in the day? I don't know. Often he is in the study when I come home in the evening. It is annoying, this *being observed*, yet I shall do my best to ignore it. I thought about moving the mirror, but it is light by the window. My mirror is round and very small. It needs all the light it can get.

This morning I got up early, raised my blind and moved around the room in half light. Coming back from the bedroom in my dressing gown, I glanced up and saw him dart across the room, naked, to the desk. His body is thin and hairy. Coyly, he covers his genitals with an A4 envelope as he hurries out. No glance in my direction.

The man has dark hair and is thirty, or older. He appears to live alone, but I cannot see the lower windows in his terrace, so it is possible that he lives in a shared house, like me, or with a lover. At the weekends, he is nearly always in his study. I don't know what he does there all day - he wants me to try and guess, but I won't give him that satisfaction.

The nights are drawing in. The blind is so thin, I fear that he can make out my shadow through it. But I can't be sure. All I know is that there are times I can feel him watching me. Today was one of them. I went to the window. As I pushed a corner of the blind aside, I thought I saw his light go off. Tonight, I asked Graham to stay the night, without telling him why. He wouldn't understand. I slept badly, not used to another presence next to mine, so I got up to write my journal. His light was out. I checked.

*

Outside it is late October. The clear, cool days are giving way to troubled autumn. Black clouds rush over the sky. When I came home tonight, he was already at his desk, staring out of the window, without the light on. His window is the first thing I look at when I come home. The others have lace curtains, to keep out intruding eyes. His bathroom (or the room that I presume is his bathroom) has them too. Do all the other windows on my side have such curtains? I have no way of knowing.

In town I hover round the shopping centre for an hour before I finally visit the stall that sells lace. A sign says 'Nets', with a list of patterns and prices. I start to talk to the woman, then I realise she will have to cut the stuff for me and I have not measured the window. But soon, any day now.

Last night I dreamt of him at his desk. I sit at the window, staring. Suddenly, he gets up, a huge piece of paper in his hand. He holds it up to the window. 'WHY DON'T YOU CALL ME?' he's written, and beneath it, a phone number. I look around for paper. I don't know what I am going to write, but when I turn back a curtain has descended between his terrace and mine, like a thin cloud, or fog. I look at the paper and read what I have written there. 'I am not on the telephone.' This is a lie.

Who can I tell about this? The others in the house are younger than me, and around less often. I know what they will say. I should have put the net curtains up months ago, as soon as I moved in. Subconsciously, they will say, I want him to watch me. I want him. But I do not. I do not.

Saturday. Maureen puts highlights in my hair. I buy a new sweater and wear my tightest jeans. At twelve, he goes into the study and begins to work. I see him glance my way, but I am beside the dresser. He can hardly see me. I check my appearance in the mirror, then stand in the window, willing him to watch. I sway backwards and forwards, as though involved in some ritual or form of exercise. I lean back like a cheap dancer, letting him take in the shape of my body. He pretends not to be looking, but every few seconds stares over, averting his eyes only when I glance in his direction.

This afternoon I bought the nets - a plain design, cut to size. I struggled to fit the hooks. They are meant to tap in, but came flying out when I connected the cord. On the third go, they held. I have left the top bit of the window, which opens, clear. If I stand on tip toes by my door, I can just see over to his room. But he cannot see me.

In the evening, his light is on, but the blind is drawn, for once. My earlier suspicions are confirmed. I can make out the outline of his desk, his lamp, just as he could see mine. But now there is a further barrier between us: white, shimmering; like a thin membrane of cloud, or a veil.

Sunday. It is so dingy that I switch the main light on to work by. Immediately, I can feel him watching me. I move to the back of the room, but can't see him from my perch on the chair. He may be too low for me, huddled over his desk. I should have bought thicker nets. I'm sure that he can see through them, see everything in my room as the light makes my curtain translucent. I have only to move the curtain aside and I shall see him, staring. I duck out of sight and prepare to swoop on the curtain, catch him. But I know he will see. I will not give him that satisfaction. Instead, I draw the blind. The nets and the blind: these will protect me!

My M.A. is falling behind - the days at the Uni seem to go so fast and I no longer feel like working at home in the evenings. Graham has met someone else, he writes to tell me; I'm glad for him. Today, one of the others in the house said 'we see so little of you, you've become like a ghost'. They think I go out all the time, but I don't, I stay in my room, with the lights off. Then, when his comes on, I can see at once. I rush to the window and peer through the bottom corner, where the nets do not quite touch. Or sometimes, I stand on tiptoes on the chair at the back of the room and watch from there. I shake so much that I think I will fall, but I never do.

His blind is down as often as it is up nowadays. He is punishing me for buying the nets. Or maybe it is because the nights are colder. The blind provides a little extra insulation. I know, because I have mine down so seldom these days, and I feel the difference. I fear he is no longer interested in me. Perhaps he never was. All sorts of doubts creep into the mind when you're in a room on your own for so long.

Where has he gone? He is in his study less and less these days, while I am in my room more and more. My blind is always up. I have moved my bed, so that it is under the window, and I can just raise my head a little, push aside the nets, and see his room. Tonight, his blind is drawn, but the light is on, and I can see his outline at his desk, working. It is enough.

The doctor came today. One of the others in the house had come to see me; something about a bill. She called him at once. He tells me I have pneumonia and must rest constantly. Also, he insists that I move my bed away from the window, but as soon as he's gone I return it there. The others in the house are solicitous. They bring me soup and drinks, though I rarely want them. The doctor must have said something. You looked up from your window today, and I think you saw me staring at you. I no longer see the need to conceal that I am looking. Quickly, you looked away.

I am recovering, the doctor tells me! It will not be necessary for me to go into hospital, but my recuperation will be slow. When he is gone, one of the others comes in as I am moving the bed back. He asks what I am doing. I am unable to explain. He asks about my family, whether there are people I can stay with. I tell him that I am not going anywhere. They still bring me soup, sometimes biscuits, but there is resentment in their eyes and I can tell they fear a relapse. If only they knew! The reason for my low spirits is that I have not seen you at the window for two whole days!

It is the coldest winter for fourteen years, one of the others tells me. She asks where I am going for Christmas. I had forgotten Christmas, and ask her to buy me cards, stamps. They are all going away, she says. Secretly, I am pleased. I do not want their frequent interruptions, their nagging inquiries after my health. I tell her I am getting better, not to worry. Actually, this is far from the truth. I am thinner and weaker. I can feel my spirit becoming vaguer, almost transparent. Only you keep me tethered to this world. Your presence, across the yards, shows me that I am real.

Christmas Day. The house is silent. Your blind is drawn. The lights are out. I venture from my room to the shower. The heating is on full and I savour being able to walk through the house naked, unfettered. When I return to my room your light is on. I switch on mine and hurry to the window, pulling my towel around me. You are in a dressing gown, leaning over the desk, a glass in one hand, which now and then you drink from. You are wrapping a last minute present.
    I watch you do this for a minute, maybe two. You are slow and clumsy. If I was there, I would do it for you. I can feel it now, feel it down to the marrow of my bones: today is the day! I pull the net curtain back so that it is behind me, willing you to look over. My bare shoulders brush against the frosted glass and tingle. You finish wrapping one present, then start another, sipping at your drink all the while. Then you finish, and stand up: presents in one hand, drink in the other.
    At last it happens! You glance at the window and see me, staring. You smile, or I think you smile, and raise your glass in greeting. I

smile back. Standing up, I let the towel fall away from me and, naked, balanced on my bed, I rip the nets from their cord and pull them round me - a cold, pure white, like a wedding dress, or a shroud.

Then I draw the blind and go downstairs.

JOSHY SLEEPING

Erika Martin

My Josh is sleeping in my arms.
The silky desert of his skin
is smoothly blowing over me
to cover my oasis.
So close now, his perfect ear
sails the millpond of his cheek,
from which his sideburn marches out,
as if a thousand iron filings
had stood to my attention.
His nose is pushing deep into
the pale folds my body makes.
His resting eye's a spider's web
of lashes, so delicate,
like inky-coloured lace.
His eyebrow is a smudge of chalk,
daubed upon his brow.
He is a country to explore,
the nation of my lover's soul.
He sleeps, as much my baby,
vulnerable within his dreams
I want to nurture:
swallow soft his angered pain.
Let him awake
renewing with my love,
yawn and sigh, then shyly rise.
Each breath of mine into his lungs
I'll blow to augment out his life.
His face, his cock, his innocence,
reworks my world, and so he solves
the quest for my repentance.

METAMORPHOSIS

Nicola Monaghan

There was a hurricane last night. It sounded like a million bees swarming round the beach hut and woke me. I walked to the window and looked through the metal mesh. The air was golden, full of sand, rubbing and grinding and causing the buzzing. I didn't feel scared, though I should have. I never thought how a gust in the wrong direction could wrench our little chalet, and the two of us, up and into the Indian Ocean. I wanted to go and look at the waves, watch the sea fight and kick and buck like a rodeo mule. I woke Ake and suggested it, but he laughed at me. Told me we'd drown in the sand. Instead I lay in bed and listened. The storm whistled and screamed for hours and, before it waned, I had fallen asleep again.

At breakfast this morning we drank tea, and ate the doughy bread and pale eggs I've grown sick of. The second restaurant, the better one, had blown away, along with several homeless types huddled there for shelter. Ake and I hardly spoke. He looked buried deep inside himself, a condemned man. I wasn't enjoying watching him worry, so I looked away. Two tables along, a pink girl had left the lid off the jam. Flies of all sizes dipped in and out of the jar.

I hate flies. They remind me of when I was younger and found a tub of maggots my dad had forgotten about. It was metamorphosis trifle. Maggots at the bottom covered by a layer of pupae, topped with flies. All dead. The higher in the jar, the further in the lifecycle. I could imagine the insects waking up and flying around, bumping into each other in a mad Brownian motion and finding no food except fly and maggot until the air ran out and they all died. The tub stunk of dead fly, a smell that hit me in the face and knocked my head back. The stench stayed with me so that I get a whiff of it every time I see a fly. It's the smell of decay, bins on a hot day.

I pointed out the pink girl and her friends to Ake. You could tell by their trendy long shorts they were on a diving trip.

"I can't believe nobody has noticed," I said.

"You did," Ake said, making me smile.

"I hate divers," I said. "And travellers too. All those jerks in Stone Town with their pork pie embroidered hats and smell of unwashed underwear."

"Who do you like then?" Ake said.

"Just us. People with no purpose who get stoned on the beach."

"And look where that got us," Ake said.

Metamorphosis

I lit a cigarette and sucked on it, put my hand on top of his. "It'll be all right," I told him. But I didn't believe it would.

John and Susie arrived then, carrying plates and more tea.

"Morning!" Susie said. She beamed, all false light and sunshine. I could see in her eyes she was faking it too. We nodded up at her. I flicked ash on the floor.

"Oh look," she said, pointing at the sea behind me. I turned and gazed past the end of her finger. Just our side of the horizon a cyclone drilled into the water. We all watched.

"The locals say that's Allah, sending the wind to scare away a shark," Ake told us.

"I wish he'd send something for the flies," I said. Everyone laughed, but it was canned laughter. More faking. We were shitting it. Underneath false cheer and jokes about flies, we were all thinking the same thing. Hoping Allah would send a strong wind. Something that could lift up all the trouble we'd got into and blow it away into the sea.

Ake and I decided to take the hire car back to Stone Town alone. No point everyone going. If things did go wrong, Susie and John could help us. Get in touch with parents, proper British lawyers, that kind of thing. Not that it would come to that, we said. Ake drove and I smoked with the window open. The road to the capital had checkpoints every five miles or so where a soldier would stop you and make you get out of the car, check you didn't stink of alcohol and had a driver's licence. I tensed as we approached the first of these and were flagged down. Then I remembered we weren't in the same danger as we had been on the journey up.

That'd been hell. After our encounter with the policeman in Stone Town, we'd shoved the joints under the leather seat covers and left. Susie had been driving and didn't notice a couple of guards waving madly for us to pull over. It'd looked like we had something to hide, which we did. All it would've needed was for one of them to follow us and give the car a proper going over. We'd been lucky.

That night we'd smoked all the joints, sitting on the sand as it cooled, watching hermit crabs burrow. I'd got head rush and imagined I was like the crabs, eyes stuck on antennae outside of my body. Ake started to giggle.

"What's funny?" I said.

"We're in deep shit."

"What's going to happen to us, Ake?" Susie had asked then.

Ake shook his head and sucked his teeth. "Don't know," he said. "But my father once got forty lashes for speeding."

"He's winding you up," I'd told Susie. But I'd looked at Ake, into his eyes. I could always tell when he was lying and he wasn't. Then I'd been brave and said I'd go back with him, the two of us would sort all the trouble out.

But I didn't feel brave now.

"Do you think they'll whip us?" I asked Ake. He didn't take his eyes off the road.

"Don't know, gorgeous. But whatever they do, it'll be nothing compared to what my ma'll do for me when I get home."

"Your mother will hurt you?"

"No. She'll never speak to me again though."

We hit a bump in the road and I was knocked into Ake, catching his arm with my cigarette. "God, sorry," I said, rubbing where I'd burnt him. "She'll calm down after a week or so."

"She won't. She'd never forgive me. It'd be like if she found out about you."

I knew what this meant because Ake had been through it with me a million times. The consequences. He could never stay with me, he'd always been straight about that. One day we'd have to break up. I treated it like dying. Sure, I knew it was going to happen, but I didn't have to think about it. Ake smiled at me. I looked away. Lit another cigarette.

Stone Town smelt of old fridges and garam masala. The call to prayer echoed through the street as we arrived.

"Aren't you going?" I said to Ake.

He raised his eyebrows at me, then frowned. "Let's get a drink," he said.

"You're going straight to Hell," I told him.

We went to the bar by the harbour. The building stretched across the waterfront, a grand colonial beast. I liked to drink gin and tonic there, imagine what it must have been like all those years ago. At the right table, I could feel the time slip underneath me. See the ladies wearing corseted dresses and complaining about the heat. The men smoking in the other room. Zanzibar had been a British Colony and, before that, German. Part of the silk route. Famous for the white slave trade, one of my friends had told me when I'd said we were going. I quite enjoyed the fantasy of being sold into a Harem. The idea of group sex and saris did something for me. I would've loved to play act this with Ake, but I knew he'd get offended and say I was being a

racist. Even though he was the only person I knew who still used the word 'Paki' in a derogatory way.
I gulped at my drink. Despite the East African heat, I shivered.
"Shall we order another one?" I said.
"No. Won't help if we reek of alcohol," Ake pointed out.

Ake parked the car outside the hire shop and we climbed out. I took a deep breath and we both stood looking at the door. He grabbed my hand and we walked towards it. I looked at my hand wrapped in his. Our eyes met and we both managed a weak smile.

"Ah. Mister Denika. We were just asking each other how long before you would come back, weren't we Raj man? You see, Raj here, he didn't think you would come back. But I told him." It was the man with the pockmarked face who said this, the one who'd persuaded the policeman to let us go the last time we were in there. He'd pointed out that he had Ake's passport, as deposit on the car, and we had to come back for it. The policeman had relented. Afterwards, Ake had convinced us all he was just after a bribe. I hoped so.

Ake said something in Swahili to the pockmarked man. They spoke for a few minutes, then Ake turned to me and said, "He says he has to get the policeman back to see us. If he doesn't they'll close him down."

"He won't take money?" I said.

Ake shook his head and looked grim. I tightened my grip on his hand. The pockmarked man picked up the phone and spoke Swahili into it. He put it down and beamed at the two of us.

"It will be all right Englishman," he said to Ake. "He'll take money off you. That's all he wants I'm sure."

"How much should we offer him?" I said.

"You'll have to ask him that," the pockmarked man said. He turned from me to the administration on his desk. I breathed.

After a couple of minutes the policeman arrived. He was wearing the same yellow baseball cap he'd had on when he caught John on the High Street. The idiot had decided to buy some joints off this dodgy bloke, right outside the Post Office in the centre of town. Anyone could have told him it was stupid. John wasn't usually dense like that.

"What do you want?" I asked the policeman. "How can we sort this out?"

He took off his yellow cap and looked me over as if he was trying to work something out. I thought it was going to be all right then, that he would come up with a figure.

"I want to arrest you and put you in prison," he told us. And behind him, through the door, came a group of uniformed officers carrying handcuffs and guns.

It's strange, to have your head held while you're pushed into a car. To feel metal against your wrists. To be in a car with men talking Swahili. I hadn't needed to come with Ake. They didn't have my passport, just his. And the only promise he'd ever made was to leave me one day. I looked at Ake, but his eyes stayed straight, focused on the seat back. I waited for him to tell them this had nothing to do with me.

But Ake said nothing.

I looked away from my boyfriend. Onto the back of the drivers seat in front on me. There was a fly, licking its legs the way they do. Spreading germs all over. I felt sick just looking at it. The smell came back to me again, the layers of dead fly at different life stages I'd found in the garage. That made me think about home, about Mum and Dad and what they'd think of all this. How they'd feel if I got whipped. Or worse, ended up in prison out here.

"It was him. He did it," I said. "My boyfriend bought lots of cannabis and hid it in the car."

The policeman turned to look at me and took out a notepad. Ake still said nothing but stared, at me, then at the fly on the back of the policeman's seat. The fly stopped licking its legs, stopped twitching on the seat, as if it could feel the weight of Ake's eyes on its back. Then it flew off, out past me and through the open window.

But I could still smell fly. It smelt like rotting flesh. Like bins on a hot day.

COMPLINE

Elaine Kazimierczuk

The schumach meanwhile, having had a little time to grow
Is yet more gorgeous.
This long hot season suits her needs.
One downpour finds the roots
That creep just underneath the earth,
The surface of the soil, reliable
That waits all summer long.
Small miracle of truth
The bliss that feeds the soul
The needless toil that makes us strong
And lovers who have wept
For spoiling love
Will make amends.
We reap not, neither do we sow,
The night prayer in the darker hours
Lends us the grace to learn to love again
And see a smile return
Beneath the shade of lovely schumach leaves
And velvet flowers
And witness the first fruits of them that slept.

SELF UNCONDEMNED

Peter Porter

Far back, forgotten mostly, parents still
Are physical and grow again in you,
Not naturally but butchered in the night
Where they're reborn; not what they are, but do;
What life they handed on, reclaimed; what place
They trumpeted; which sentences they knew
Would sting at last, sans portent or proviso.

The nights are full of talk of death which sounds
In no way like true death, but just chit-chat
Of the body's winsomeness. Where's terror
Which took Bible names, Jehosophat,
Jehu? Which silence of geography
Set floods to streak the shining funeral ghats?
Exchange rate, Heaven to catastrophe.

And still showing on the screen, "Nothingness may be
Redeemed by Nothing." You will go back where
You have no sense of having ever been -
Therefore you crave forgiveness, and despair
At being what you are. The ant warps to
Its home, always in arms, in millions rare,
A movement of the census, seeming more.

GABBRO

Marcus Saban

"*Madainn mhath!*"

He'd only just fallen asleep, and now he was being woken again. He tried to move inside the sleeping bag, but was held too tightly by the olive green bivvy bag that encased it. He struggled an arm out and unzipped the condensation-damp material across his face. The sun came right in at him and he screwed his eyes shut again. There was laughter, a female chuckle, and a deeper, gruffer voice, the Gaelic repeated in English.

"Good morning there."

He opened his eyes again. Paul MacNicol, the mountain guide whose name was really Pòl MacNeacail, was sitting over an alpine stove boiling some water. Ishbel was already stuffing her rolled up sleeping bag into her rucksack.

"Come on Rob, day's half gone already."

Rob looked at his watch. Five a.m.

"Aye laddie," Paul added. "Been daylight for hours now. There's some porridge here, and I'm just getting a brew on. Be needing it today." There was a large plastic camping bowl with a spoon in it sitting by the little red gas bottle that fed the stove.

Rob heaved himself out of the green maggot-like bivvy, grunting with the effort. His elbow landed on the hard grey-brown rock, then his hip, and finally he was able to kick the thing off his legs. It flopped sideways, stretched out by the orange self-inflating foam mattress inside. He wore a black close-fitting hat, a long-sleeved Helly Hansen vest, stretchy thermal bottoms, and a pair of fleecy-lined things that weren't quite shoes and weren't quite socks – and certainly weren't suitable for standing on hard rock with a surface like sandpaper. He sat on the empty green cocoon to change them for thick socks and a pair of heavy boots.

Then he realised how cold he was. It might be early June and sunny, but 2900 feet up on Skye this hour of the day there was a deep chill, and he shivered until he could pull on his black windproof fleece.

"Hurry up, it's good stuff," Ishbel said, inclining her head toward the porridge. "Plenty of honey."

Paul poured boiling water into three titanium mugs. Rob stopped rubbing his hands together and picked up the porridge. It certainly was good, and warming too.

As he ate, he looked around. The view was spectacular, he couldn't blame his late father-in-law for saving this ridge till last. He just wished he hadn't died before he could do it, and then Ishbel wouldn't be here doing it instead, dragging Rob along with her.

He wasn't a bad sort really, Norman. Like Paul, another native of this island, he too had anglicised his name. Tormod MacDòmhnall became Norman MacDonald. And he used to call Rob "Laddie" too, even into his thirties.

Ish was still suffering with the loss. That was what this expedition was about. A full traverse of the Cuillin Ridge, the only Munros Norman hadn't climbed since retiring from the Marines and becoming a postman down in Plymouth. He'd been saving them for last, finishing on the island of his birth, but illness prevented him. And at the end, on the slopes of Sgurr nan Gillean, Ish was to scatter his ashes. She had them in her rucksack, so in a way Norman was doing the ridge with them.

Eleven Munros. Eleven mountains over 3000 feet joined by a broken knife-edge of a ridge, in one day.

Paul placed a mug of tea beside Rob, and began pointing out the scenery. They were on the narrow saddle between the jagged peaks of Gars-Bhein and Sgurr a Choire Bhig, having slogged up from the lush greenery of Glen Brittle the day before. To the south was the sea, nearby the twin linked islets of Soay, further off Canna, Rum, Eigg and Muck. Apparently the Gaelic name for Muck meant Isle of Pigs. He'd been to the Isle of Dogs once when he was in CID to arrest someone, but that seemed far away now.

To the east was the shadow-streaked bulk of Bla Bheinn, the island's twelfth Munro and Norman's first; to the north-east, the blue pool of Loch Coruisk; beyond that, the pale and lonely hump of Marsco. And, all around them and towering above, the dark savagery of the Cuillin Ridge.

"And there of course," Paul said, pointing to a great grey point that stuck straight up into the sky above the rest, "is Sgurr nan Gillean. After that, we'll head down the south-east ridge and along to the Sligachan Hotel for a wee dram. Something to keep in mind as we work our way along. It's only seven miles, but it'll take all day, and there are few escape routes, none of them easy." He looked them each in the eye from the top his mug. "You're sure about this?"

"I have to do it," Ishbel said.

"Aye, but d'you have the climbing experience?"

Rob replied. "We did the Aonach Eagach in Glen Coe a few weeks ago."

He didn't mention how he froze on the pinnacles, two thousand feet on either side, Ish desperately trying to talk him across while another group waited behind.

"Hmm." Paul nodded. "The narrowest on the mainland, but this one's harder. OK, if we stick together and you do as I say, we'll be fine." He knocked back the rest of his tea and stood up to pack everything away. "In fact, we're very lucky. The forecast's like this all day. Can be pretty *driech* up here most times. What was it like on the Aonach Eagach?"

"Pretty *driech*," Ish replied. Born in Plymouth, she had little of her father's accent, but she still used plenty of Scots expressions. Those and the ones from the Royal Marines, like calling food scran, and going to the head instead of the toilet. Jean, her well-to-do Devon-born mother, never quite approved of that sort of language. She should hear some of the other things Ish came out with.

Paul was pulling his gear together, a mass of rope, harnesses and metal attachments dangling from a sling. Time to nip behind a rock for a moment before departure.

The highest point. Rob could feel his heart hammering against his ribs with more than just the exertion of the hard pull up the slope. Ish too was catching her breath.

"Named after Alexander Nicolson," Paul was saying. "Did all sorts of things, finished up Sheriff of Greenock. But most famous on Skye for having Sgurr Alasdair named after him. He was the first to climb it, in 1873. Don't think he was a relative of mine, the genealogy of the Nicolsons and the MacNicols is complicated. But he was an Uncle of Sorley MacLean, the poet."

Ish, who had taken a photograph earlier and was now chewing on a cereal bar, looked up at the mention of the name, then picked up her water bottle and took a long pull. Rob knew he should eat something too, but his appetite was gone. The drop down into the narrow gap at the top of the Great Stone Chute, a near-vertical waterfall of rocks and scree, was making it difficult to swallow. Paul was unfurling some rope, digging out harnesses and fitting metal things together.

To delay the moment when he would have to pull the plastic helmet out of his sack, Rob started fiddling with his compass.

"Wouldn't bother with that, laddie," Paul said. "Get all sorts of false readings here. This is gabbro–" he stamped his boot on the rock "– volcanic magnetite. Magnetic. That's why people like me stay in business."

Then he pointed to the thing Rob had managed to avoid noticing. "Over there's Sgurr Dearg, the Inaccessible Pinnacle – the In Pin." There it was, a huge grey-brown fin, leaning slightly to one side. The only Munro that could not be climbed without mountaineering skills.

Ish chose not to notice Rob's pale complexion, but Paul saw it. "Sure you're all right with this? There's an escape route below. I can take the two of you off here, down the Stone Chute."

Rob said there was no problem, but paused just a moment too long. Ishbel flared up. "Look come on for Christ's sake, Rob. It's OK. You've got to fight it. Dad did it, I can do it, and you never had any problem in the Peaks. What's the matter?"

Paul raised an eyebrow. The Peak District bore little resemblance to these mountains. Ish turned to him. "He had no trouble standing on top of the Trinnacle. Even jumped from one side to the other."

"Look, I'll be all right, OK?"

"I know the Trinnacle," Paul said. "Two fingers of rock sticking out over the valley. You'll be fine with this wee abseil. Getting up the other side's tricky, but we'll do it. At least it's dry. This bit's basalt, skitie as soap in the wet. And it's a weekday too, so no crowds. Some days you're queuing up."

Rob pulled himself up, ready for the descent into the dark gulley between the peaks. He ignored the steep fall of broken rocks below. The more this ridge threw at him, the more determined he became to beat it.

The worst point. The absolute worst. Paul was already on top, holding the rope as Ish crawled up toward him. It was ridiculous. How could a rock formation like this exist? The way it leaned to the left, surely a couple more storms and it would fall over, crashing into the grey-brown wilderness so far below.

Paul was giving words of encouragement as she inched along. It wasn't even a foot wide higher up, and a two thousand foot drop.

Sgurr Dearg, pronounced 'Jerrack'. The Red Peak, second highest. Rob's ears were full of heartbeat and his hands shook. Once again he checked his harness and made sure his helmet was on right. He was starting to feel cold.

He knew what the trouble was – what had started it. A young, semi-homeless crack-addicted street thief who said he was eighteen and they chose to believe him because it saved time, even though they knew he was more like sixteen. They hadn't wanted some social worker sitting there in the interview room, they wanted him to sign a statement incriminating his dealer.

The DS Rob was assisting hoped the dealer would give something away about his supplier, and so on up the tree – and the promotion ladder. Except it had gone wrong. The lad got a beating for being a grass, then tried to steal another handbag. He got a vicious kicking from the woman's boyfriend and died a few hours later in intensive care.

The DS moved to another district in disgrace, and Rob requested a move back into uniform – Traffic, where now every RTA filled him with dread at what he might have to deal with. No way for a copper to be, no way at all.

"*Your turn!*" Ish shouted down to him as she disappeared over the far edge on an abseil.

It seemed OK. Plenty of handholds, lots of grip on the coarse rock. Like Paul had said, it was graded 'moderate', meaning 'easy'. It was just the exposure. But he was moving. Like Ish, he was moving slowly up toward Paul.

"Keep looking at me," he was saying, "and you'll have no trouble at all." He kept the rope taught, slowly pulling it in as Rob moved.

Then he reached the narrowest point, ten inches across and a sheer drop each side. He was lying face down along its length. How could he not look down? He could feel the panic rising. He no longer felt the hard gabbro beneath him. The blade of rock was leaning like the Tower of Pisa, and there was nothing beneath him, nothing at all. He could feel himself going, rolling off the top...

Paul was talking, calmly, smoothly. Telling him to look straight at him, not to panic, this happens to lots of people. Remember I've got the rope, tied securely round the big rock beside me, you're quite safe. Just look at me...

But Rob was elsewhere, in an arc-lit world of blue lights, a pile-up on the M1 near Hucknall, three teenagers dead in a stolen Fiat sideswiped by a Polish artic, blood all over what was left of the car's interior. The artic's driver slammed on the air brakes and a tail-gating BMW smacked into the back, two occupants receiving urgent treatment in one of the ambulances. Like a battle scene, and none of the lads old enough even for a moped.

"*Rob!*" He heard Ish's voice, faint from way over the other side, somewhere beneath Paul.

"All right, Ishbel," Paul said, never taking his eyes from Rob, "don't worry. Rob's just a wee bit fast on the ridge. I'm going to help him along a little."

He fastened his belay to the tall boulder and crawled along to Rob, who looked up as he approached.

"OK lad, OK. Now, see this lump of rock here..." Paul guided Rob's hand onto the next handhold, patiently coaxing him along. He knew every handhold, every foothold, and quietly, almost tenderly, talked him through it.

They made it. Rob couldn't believe it, he was shaking as he pulled himself upright against the boulder so Paul could ready him for the abseil.

Paul patted him on the shoulder. "Well done, laddie, well done."

Rob worked his way backwards down onto the main slope of Sgurr Dearg. Norman said the Marines used to do this forwards, straight over cliffs. "Very good for rapid evacuations!"

And Ish was at the bottom, hugging him and making all sorts of noises of relief.

"God, Rob, I couldn't see what was happening. You were up there ages."

Rob couldn't reply.

Paul arrived beside them, shaking the rope loose and coiling it up.

"Nothing to worry about," he said. "Just a little crag fast, that's all. Happens to everyone. Even to me, but don't tell anyone, eh?" He winked, and cracked his weather beaten face into a broad grin.

Rob separated himself from Ish and blew his nose.

"Right then," said Paul. "Six more before we head home, best get going. You'll be pleased to hear they're a little easier now."

Rob pulled a cereal bar out of his pocket and followed the others along the rough path.

The last one, and it wasn't easy at all. Sgurr nan Gillean, Peak of the Young Men. Fatigue was worsening and it was getting late. The light was starting to dim, yet Rob could still appreciate the spectacular views as he approached the near vertical scramble to the tiny summit.

Finally they reached it, standing beside the small cairn. The closest parts were invisible from the peak, so it seemed they were hanging in the sky. The Sligachan Hotel was just visible to the north, and in the opposite direction the whole ridge, right back to the first one, curled round like a broken question mark. Paul pointed to the island of Raasay to the west. "Where the poet was born."

"And from here it's downhill and home," Ish said, thumbs easing the straps of her rucksack.

"Aye, light's going. Best press on. I've a dram of Talisker waiting in the Sligachan." Then he remembered something and gently placed his hand on her arm. "And you've a wee task to carry out, yes?"

Ish nodded. She had not forgotten the presence of her father's ashes in her pack, or the book of Gaelic poetry that sat beside the urn. They began the difficult scramble down onto the south-east ridge.

They were on the lower slopes of Sgurr na h-Uamha, the lowest of the subsidiary peaks, still loose and rocky but close to the boggy green and black of Harta Corrie, the River Sligachan below. The sun had set somewhere behind the sharp teeth of Sgurr na Banachdich – 'Smallpox Peak' – and they were now in shadow.

Ish dug into her rucksack and pulled out first a copy of *From Wood to Ridge*, which she handed to Rob. Then she pulled out her father's pewter urn. Rob had been surprised at the weight of it. He had not expected a quantity of ashes to weigh so much.

He looked at Ish. Still no tears, just the look of determination she had worn at the funeral. Paul, maintaining a discreet distance, noticed the book but said nothing.

Ish nodded to Rob, and he turned to a page marked with a yellow post-it note. He started to read, and Ish removed the lid of the container. A slight breeze had picked up, blowing down from the north, and the ashes of Tormod MacDòmhnall, native of *Eilean Sgitheanach*, were picked up and blown across the mighty curving ridge.

"'*An Cuillithionn*,'" Rob began, and he continued with a passage from MacLean's epic poem, and in Gaelic. Paul stared open-mouthed, and Ish was forced to turn her head as he continued. The last time she heard Sorley MacLean – Somhairle MacGill-Eain – in the original was the last time she saw her father, a whispered few lines from *Hallaig*.

Rob read the short passage they had agreed. When they were finished and Norman's ashes were scattered across the Cuillin Ridge, they stood for a minute, and Rob saw tears on Ishbel's cheeks. Presently she put her head on his shoulder. He enfolded her in his arms.

"Where—" she began.

"From a book," he replied. "From a book."

After a moment, Paul decided to join them.

"Very good, Rob," he said. "Very good indeed. Slight accent, but for an Englishman I'd never have believed it."

They finished their water and continued down toward the muddy path to Sligachan. "Last of the rock," Paul said. "Interesting stuff, gabbro. Lot of it on the Moon…"